Praise for *Broken Crown*

"A mirror for the human spirit. *Broken Crown* reflects the condition inside each of us living by comparison, as generation after generation chooses to put trust and hope in earthly idols and power when we have the offer of an abundant life following the simple invitation of a loving God."

> *Joby Martin*
> *Lead Pastor of The Church of Eleven22*
> *Jacksonville, FL*

"Chris has given the world an incredible gift in this book on leadership. He has not only been teaching these truths for years, but he lives a life of healthy leadership. I not only highly endorse the book, I highly endorse the leader who wrote it!"

> *Shawn Lovejoy*
> *CEO of Courage to Lead*

"*Broken Crown* is packed with both practical and biblical insights to help us avoid the quicksand in life that we often don't see until it's nearly too late. Chris Bell helps you gain deep truth from the story of King Saul that results in freedom to be the best version of you and realize your fullest potential. This book will help bring peace, wholeness, and strength to your soul."

Dan Reiland
Executive Pastor of 12Stone Church
Lawrenceville, GA

"We all want a king. It is a natural human desire to want something extraordinary that we can give our lives to and find meaning in. In his new book *Broken Crown*, Chris Bell uses the story of King Saul to shine a light on the destructive temptation to choose something besides God to rule our lives."

Carey Nieuwhof
Founding Pastor of Connexus Church and Author of Didn't See It Coming

"One of our finest young pastors and a protégé has written an interesting book on a person not often written about. His insights into King Saul are relevant and refreshing. We can learn much from the characters in the Old Testament and this book will certainly aid our journey."

James Merrit
Pastor of CrossPointe Church, Atlanta, GA
Former President of the Southern Baptist Convention

"So many people in our generation avoid the tough inner work that leads to lasting joy and fulfillment. Chris goes deep while bringing to light this fascinating biblical story! His work shines light on so many ancient practical truths that need to be shared in the 21st century!"

Andy Wood of Echo Church

"Chris gives powerful insight on how Saul can be found, not just in the pages of Scripture, but in each of us. Saul's story laid out in *Broken Crown* causes us to examine what lies beneath the surface in ourselves. *Broken Crown* shows how the little things in our lives can keep us from the big plans of God."

Kris Dolberry
Pastor of The Bridge Church
Nashville, TN

"Pastor Chris Bell sheds new light and perspective on the tragic story of Saul while helping each of us discover the struggles keeping us from reaching our God-given potential."

Frank Bealer
CEO of Phase Family Centers; Executive Director of Leadership Development at Orange; Author of The Myth of Balance

"*Broken Crown* is a journey through the often forgotten story of King Saul. It is a truthful look at the life of a man whose potential is often lost in the shadow of his struggles. Chris Bell helps us find ourselves in this journey and reminds us that it is the little things over time that often create the greatest impact of success or failure."

Chris Brown
Former nationally syndicated radio host of Life, Money and Hope at Ramsey Solutions

"This is the rarely-told story of Saul and the nation of Israel. Chris Bell uses his unique gift as a pastoral teacher to unpack a multitude of valuable lessons for Christ-followers. Readers will be compelled to examine the condition of their own heart and use the biblical truths presented in *Broken Crown* to reveal the tremendous potential we each possess when we choose to walk 'under the canopy of God's authority.' Pastor Bell has created a powerful and transformative message."

Kimberly B. Leousis
Senior Director of Institutional Research
University of Mobile

"This engaging book is a much needed, self-examining walk through the life of King Saul. Chris Bell does a magnificent job of paralleling the many struggles of King Saul with the modern day battles we face each day as Christians."

Joel Goff
Sigma Southeast Sales Manager

"Chris Bell's insights from the life of Saul have the ability to change the course of your life. There is some of Saul in all of us. Let us be honest with ourselves. Glean the learnings from this story and let us become the people God has created us to be."

Raul Palacios
Executive Pastor of Church by the Glades
Fort Lauderdale, FL

"So thankful for the way God is using my friend Chris Bell and thrilled for this next step on the journey as a writer. His insights into the life of King Saul and the application he brings from the Old Testament narrative to the story of our lives today are masterful. You will definitely want to read this book and I promise God will teach you profound modern lessons from this tragic ancient story."

Vance Pitman
Senior Pastor of Hope Church
Las Vegas, NV

"As a pastor, I am really grateful that Pastor Chris Bell has written *Broken Crown*. I have never preached on the life of King Saul mainly because I never knew where to start, or how to make it applicable to my congregation. Now, I have no excuse! The Lord has been kind in laying this on the heart of my friend Chris Bell, and pastors like myself and the congregations we lead will benefit greatly from this work on the important story that is the life and rule of King Saul."

Dean Inserra
Pastor of City Church
Tallahassee, FL

Broken Crown: Ancient Tragedy, Modern Lessons

Publisher: 3Circle Church (April 7, 2019)
Language: English
ISBN-10: 0578470950
ISBN-13: 978-0578470955

Editor: Stephanie Glines
Cover Design: Live Design
Formatting and Layout: Peppermedia

BROKEN CROWN

ANCIENT TRAGEDY · MODERN LESSONS

CHRIS BELL

This book is dedicated to the legacy and memory of my grandparents, Kenneth and Barbara Bell. On a rural farm in coastal Mississippi, Pop and Nanny created an environment full of love, commitment, and family. Most of all, they pointed me to Jesus. I will forever be grateful for the influence they had in shaping me to be the man I am today.

Foreword

It's a cliché we've all heard and quickly nod our heads in agreement with: *A great start is no guarantee of a happy ending.* But if truth be known, all of us prefer a great start—because we think our story will be different.

We love it when our favorite team rushes out to a big lead, even though time after time that big lead disappears when overconfidence and sloppy play leads to a massive change in momentum.

The same goes for those of us that are entrepreneurs or church planters. We're elated after a successful grand opening. We're certain that it portents a great future.

Or have you noticed how parents and family members tend to assume that the Little League All-Star will one day get a D-1 scholarship; the most popular kid in elementary school will grow up to be mayor; and the "wild child" will end up in jail somewhere.

It's human nature. We all assume that whoever has the best start, the best resources, and the best skills wins the race. But that's not how life works. The journey is far more important than the start. And the finish is all that really matters.

In *Broken Crown*, Chris Bell takes us back to one of the best starts in biblical history, the coronation of King Saul, and then shows us how this incredible start became a horrific ending.

It's a story that has too often been overlooked. Granted, King Saul has become a well-known caricature of failure. In the pantheon of biblical heroes, he's a certified bum. But while many know his failure, few have ever stopped to consider why and how it happened.

And that's where this book makes a significant contribution. It fills a serious gap. It's not a history lesson. It's a well-crafted series of insights and life lessons that speak to the King Saul in all of us. The fact is, whether you're a brand-new Jesus follower or the most seasoned saint in the church, the spiritual pitfalls and danger zones we face are pretty much the same. The things that derailed King Saul still derail us today.

When it comes to biblical narratives and books like this (and the Bible itself), I find that most of us tend to fall into one of two camps. Some of us treat the information we learn as a God-given pair of binoculars. We apply it to others, making a mental list of who needs to hear what, and who needs to seriously clean up their act. But others realize that it's supposed to be used as a mirror, carefully noting the things they see in themselves that need to be cleaned up, altered, or realigned with Scripture.

My hope is that you will read and use this book as a mirror, letting the forgotten story of Saul's demise speak to the path you're currently taking. Read it carefully and reflect deeply. Because when a man who essentially started life on third base never reaches home, there are important lessons to be learned no matter where we are in our walk with Jesus.

Larry Osborne
Author and Pastor of North Coast Church
Vista, CA

Introduction

His heart pounded in his chest. Beads of sweat dripped from the tip of his nose and dotted the sandy soil where his sandaled feet now stood. No matter how hard he tried, he couldn't stop his hands and knees from shaking. The sound of the massive crowd chanting his name rushed over him like a tsunami of dreams and demands. They want a king, and he is their man.

It had never been easy for Saul to hide. At 30 years old, he was the tallest and most handsome man in the nation of Israel. No one looked the part of a valiant leader more than Saul did.

But here he is—the future King of Israel and God's chosen leader—hiding behind a pile of baggage and equipment. He can hear the prophet Samuel as he calls the nation together. Like a roaring crowd before a concert, the clamor was deafening and only added to the fear that drove him to this hiding spot in the first place. This crowd had assembled for *him*. Saul had been noticed, admired, and even revered for much of his life. But today was different. The crowd waiting for him today brought not only adoration but expectations as well—lots of them. And Saul was simply not ready to carry the weight of that responsibility.

In a few moments, God Himself will lead Samuel to Saul's hiding place, pulling him out from behind the baggage to take his place as Israel's first king. And with what feels like the weight of the nation on his shoulders, Saul's reign begins and one of the most fascinating and devastating stories in the Bible starts to unfold.

Understandably, but unfortunately, it's a story that is often overlooked, covered in the dust storm left behind by the epic tales of Samuel's prophetic leadership and King David's victorious reign. There have been countless books written and sermons preached on these two men—but not Saul.

My purpose in writing *Broken Crown* is to shed some light on this too often neglected biblical narrative and the valuable lessons we can learn from it. You see, if we're honest, I believe we have more in common with King Saul than we realize. In fact, as you read through this book, don't be surprised if the person on the page starts to look familiar.

A man full of promise who fails time and time again to live up to his God-given potential.

A man with an impressive façade masking a dark inner reality that will ultimately lead to a tragic fall.

Sound like anyone you know? No, I don't mean the person down the street. I'm talking about me and you. I'm talking about the "King Saul" staring back at us in the mirror each morning. I'm talking about the struggles within our own heart we're forced to confront every single day. As we take a deeper look into this ancient account, I encourage you to let King Saul's story inform your story. He has so many lessons to teach us.

Chapter One
An Environment for Disaster

[4] Then all the elders of Israel gathered together and came to Samuel at Ramah and said to him, "Behold, you are old and your sons do not walk in your ways. [5] Now appoint for us a king to judge us like all the nations." (1 Samuel 8:4-5 ESV)

It was April of 1912. The massive steamship was proudly cruising at high speed through the frigid iceberg-infested waters of the northern Atlantic. Unparalleled in size and luxury at the time and propelled by cutting-edge technology, the Titanic was simply amazing. More than 2,200 passengers boarded this floating palace for an experience like no other—wealthy businessmen and dignitaries, celebrities and socialites, emigrants hoping for a new life on the other shore, and, of course, Leonardo DiCaprio and Kate Winslet.[1] It seemed the whole world watched with anticipation as the celebrated White Star ocean liner set sail on its maiden voyage from Southampton to New York.

As often happens with humans, those involved in the design and sailing of the Titanic were overconfident in their product and its capability. History tells us that warnings of ice and danger were ignored to embrace speed and risk.[2] Provisions for the safety of the passengers were neglected in order to cut costs and create an illusion of invincibility. What was expected to be an inevitable celebratory arrival on the American shore was suddenly and violently stopped by an iceberg. Sadly, with more people aboard the ship than lifeboats to hold them, the wonder of the maritime world barreled toward a horrific end.

The tricky thing about an iceberg is that the most dangerous part of the obstruction is hidden from view. It was estimated that the chunk of ice that caused the Titanic to sink was eight times the size of what was visible above the waterline.[3] And, in the case of you and me, it's often the things concealed beneath the surface that have the potential to cause the wreckage in our own lives.

Accounts of what happened that fateful night are varied, and who or what set in motion the events that led to the Titanic's sinking are still debated today. Multiple factors—weather conditions, recklessness and neglect, ambition and greed—all seemed to play a part. It was a perfect storm of circumstances that ultimately led to the historic tragedy.

Similarly, that's where we find the nation of Israel during the time of Samuel and Saul—in an environment ripe for a disaster. More than 1,500 people lost their lives on a sinking ship over a century ago, and the ancient pages of the Old Testament show that a generation of God's people would suffer under a broken crown.[4]

Let's set the stage with a quick recap.

The story of the Israelites is a rollercoaster ride for the ages. The book of Genesis tells the story of Abraham and his unique relationship with the Living God.[5] God made a covenant with Abraham that a great nation would be born of his seed. He promised to personally guide and bless these people. The point of this relationship was never to show how special Israel was, but to ultimately show the goodness and faithfulness of God. God would one day pave the way for redemption for the whole world through this group of ordinary humans. While the Messiah would eventually march into human history through the family tree of Abraham, the journey to that blessed kept promise would be one full of both stunning victories and crushing defeats.

God's people will eventually end up in Egyptian slavery for several hundred years. God hears the cries of his people in their captivity and orchestrates a divine rescue plan under the leadership of another ordinary man named Moses. With the Red Sea in front of them and the Egyptian army in pursuit, God miraculously parts the water for the Israelites to safely escape to the other side.[6]

While God used Moses to lead the people to freedom, it was abundantly clear that the one true God was their rescuer. Now, with the army of an empire swallowed up in the sea behind them, the Israelites had the opportunity to live under the rule and reign of a loving and faithful King. Cruel whips and empty work now gave way to loving direction and a life of hope and purpose. Begrudging compliance was replaced with affectionate obedience. A brutal tyrant was replaced by a caring Father. God proved to be their provider in the wilderness, raining down bread from heaven.[7] He proved to be their defender when He fought the battle for them at Jericho.[8] Over and over again, God showed His people that He was their great and good King. So great, in fact, that it's almost unimaginable they would ever ask for anything more.

Unfortunately, humans have a propensity to choose the rough waters of arrogant independence over the safe and smooth streams of humble submission.

[THE TRAGIC REQUEST]

Appoint for us a king… (1 Samuel 8:5 ESV)

If you live long enough, you learn that sometimes a question has more attached to it than meets the eye. A child's request for "one more story" could simply be a delaying of bedtime. A teenager's request for hang time with his parents could be an excuse to avoid cleaning his room. We've all been guilty of these mostly benign deceptions. Although this human tendency is common and often harmless, it has the potential for serious repercussions, as we're about to see.

In 1 Samuel 8:5, we find where the elders of Israel made a loaded request of their own: they wanted a different leadership model. Samuel was the last in a line of leaders God had appointed called *judges*. This prophet had been a steady hand on the wheel of the nation as he led with boldness and wisdom. It stunned and stung him to hear the representatives of the people ask for an earthly king.

One glaring omission on the part of these leaders is any exploration of the possibility that their request is flawed. They are face-to-face with one of the wisest leaders in their nation's history, yet they fail to ask Samuel for his input. As Scripture warns against over and over, they became wise in their own eyes.

These poignant words in Proverbs ring true:

There is a way that seems right to a man, but its end is the way to death. (Proverbs 14:12 ESV)

One of the greatest displays of arrogance on our part as mere mortals is to fully trust in our own wisdom. The man who claims to be simply "trusting his gut" may very well end up following his gut right over a cliff.

The gut-level instincts of Israel's appointed leaders were gut-level wrong.

Like Israel, we often fail to tap into the wisdom to which we've been given access. Too many times, we make rash decisions based on our emotions and "instincts" without consulting God's Word and asking for sound advice from trusted people in our lives. We make choices that seem like a good idea in the moment but often carry long-lasting and far-reaching consequences.

The leaders of Israel didn't ask for Samuel's counsel on the matter because they knew what he'd say, and they simply did not want to hear it. Could it be that the reason many of us stay in patterns of destructive choices is that we willingly choose to avoid the very sources of truth we desperately need?

[THE DECEPTION]

Behold, you are old and your sons do not walk in your ways. (1 Samuel 8:5 ESV)

The Israelites offered a convincing and logical reason for requesting an earthly king. *Samuel was getting old! The job was becoming too stressful for him. His sons were no comparison to him in his greatness.*

The leaders positioned themselves as only wanting the best for their aging leader and their beloved country. They attempted to both compliment him and point out what must have been a frustrating parental disappointment on his part.

Here's the thing about rebellion. Oftentimes, our disobedience is camouflaged with good intentions because the reality is too dark to reveal. The father who says leaving his family will be better for the kids in the long run is often chasing a personal fantasy life of his own. The woman who habitually overspends on her children claims she's only trying to give them the life she never had, while in reality she's trying to impress her friends.

The truth is, our hearts are fertile ground for the infestation of weeds and thorns like selfishness, insecurity, bitterness, and pride. What we're about to see is that Israel's seemingly well-meaning request was a cover-up for a much deeper heart defect. They had fallen into a snare that we modern day rebels are susceptible to as well—the trap of comparison.

[THE REALITY]

Now appoint for us a king to judge us like all the nations. (1 Samuel 8:5 ESV)

Sometimes, if you listen closely, people will tell you what's actually behind their deception. The truth tends to leak. No sooner had the Israelites offered justification for their request than they reveal their actual motive.

Why did they want an earthly king? *Because all of the surrounding nations had one! They wanted to be like everyone else.* Even though God was the perfect King for them, they could not be satisfied or rest in His care and provision.

Before you jump to judging our ancient friends, just picture this for a moment. Countless times, they'd been asked by their neighbors, "So who is your king exactly?" I'm sure that was a tough one to explain. Israel had a King alright, but He was unique to say the least. He was the all-powerful but *invisible* King. He was the mighty but *mysterious* King. He was to be followed but also to be worshipped. The Israelites had become exhausted with explaining the uniqueness of their King. Why were they so afraid to be different? What blinded them to the amazing and wonderful situation they enjoyed with their God?

Comparison and peer pressure are powerfully destructive forces. And, unfortunately, our intense desire to "follow the crowd" doesn't end when we walk across a stage to receive a diploma. Comparison continues to morph, and often intensify, as we grow older. In many ways, adults are just kids with more money and better toys. We teach our children to be secure and avoid comparison, but we fall into the same trap.

The gratitude for our home can dissipate as soon as we visit a friend's new house with more square footage and the latest custom furnishings. We're perfectly content with our car until a buddy stops by in his shiny new four-wheel drive truck with all the bells and whistles. Suddenly, we're feeling a little dissatisfied.

Sadly, the venom of this pattern of thinking can seep into the bloodstream of our human relationships. We begin to compare our spouse to another's instead of cherishing the uniqueness of the mate God has given us to love. We secretly keep score of the successes and failures of our own kids versus our friend's kids.

Comparison was the driving factor behind one of

the most disastrous decisions in Israel's history. It caused them to choose a flawed earthly king over a perfect heavenly one. And if we're not careful, it can lead to our own broken kingdom as well.

While the Israelites attempted to keep up their thin charade, God was ready to call a spade a spade.

[THE SIN]

And the Lord said to Samuel, "Obey the voice of the people in all that they say to you, for they have not rejected you, but they have rejected me from being king over them." (1 Samuel 8:7 ESV)

To place our ultimate trust and hope in something or someone other than God is a form of idolatry and a rejection of Him. We should always beware of any decision we make without God as the guiding force behind it. The Israelites thought they were making a simple governmental change, but God knew the real change was in the condition of their hearts. They didn't see it as *removing* God; they just wanted an earthly king, too. They weren't saying He wasn't a *good* King, just that He wasn't *enough*. What they viewed as merely an expansion of leadership, God viewed as a replacement of His own.

Make no mistake—the way we view things will determine how we do things. Israel's blindness to the relationship they experienced under the one true King's loving rule led them to abandon the leadership that had sustained them.

What's clear throughout Scripture is that a divided heart is no heart at all for God. In the New Testament, Jesus tells us that we can't serve two masters.[9] Like Israel, every human heart has a throne, and someone or something is going to sit on it. God alone was worthy to sit on Israel's throne, and He alone is worthy to sit on ours. We must, by the empowering of the Holy Spirit, become sensitive to the nuanced movements of our hearts and guard them carefully. What may seem to be a harmless sidestep can potentially lead to years of disappointment and regret when we walk out from under the canopy of God's authority.

[THE LESSON]

Do not be conformed to this world... (Romans 12:2 ESV)

This ancient account holds an important modern lesson. The best possible life we can experience is under the total rule and reign of God.

Israel will come to painfully regret their request for an earthly king. With Saul on the throne, the nation will soon experience the perils of placing power in the hands of an insecure, angry, and disobedient man. While they could have remained under the perfect leadership and authority of God as King, the Israelites will suffer dearly because of Saul's weaknesses.

This same principle holds true for us today. Just like

Israel, we have a choice to make. Will we embrace the wise and loving commands of our God or will we demand our independence and the impending consequences? Will we learn from the mistakes of our ancient friends or will we blaze new trails of rebellion and cause a difficult trek for the next generation?

The problem we face as humans is that submitting to authority initially feels confining to us. (Remember those teenage years?) Like a bird trapped in a cage, we long for the opportunity to glide on the breezes of perceived freedom and independence. But the reality is we're all confined to some form of authority in our lives. Some live controlled by the opinions of other people, while others live bound by wounds from the past or paralyzed by fear of the future. We're all driven by something. And, if it's not God, it will eventually lead us to a place of bondage and rob us from the life we were meant to live.

The unique and glorious thing about God's authority is that we experience the most freedom when we live under His rule in our lives. Jesus talks about this great paradox in the Gospels when He boldly calls us to die to ourselves in order to find true life.[10]

He once painted a picture of life as a choice between two gates—one narrow and one wide. Most people will choose the wide gate because it seems to be the easier path. It doesn't cost anything. The deception of the wide gate is realized only after hearing the creak of its rusty hinges as it slams shut behind you. Scripture tells us the wide gate leads to destruction. It leads to a suffocating place of endless consequences and regrets. Ironically, the wide gate leads to a very narrow place.

The narrow gate, on the other hand, is the one that leads to the wide, open space of abundant life. It's the path of God's authority and plan. It leads to purpose and fulfillment rather than emptiness and discontentment. It leads to hope rather than despair. It leads to joy rather than sorrow. It leads to freedom and to the best that God has for us. May we be among the few who find it.

The news of the Titanic tragedy headlined papers around the world. Reports from the inquiry that followed left many wondering why numerous warnings had been ignored and precautions never taken. The maritime industry would make crucial changes that are still in place to this day.[11] Getting on a boat is exponentially safer now because the people of the early 1900s learned from and applied the painful lessons of the sinking of the great ship.

In Romans 15:4, the apostle Paul writes that the stories of the Old Testament were recorded to teach us. The nation of Israel had to experience the consequence of stepping out from under God's authority firsthand, suffering decades under a broken crown. Will we be wise enough to heed the warnings from the pages of the past?

Chapter 2
Little Things Become Big Things

[10]Then the word of the Lord came to Samuel, [11]"I regret that I made Saul king, for he has turned away from following me and has not carried out my instructions." (1 Samuel 15:10-11 NIV)

On November 20, 2016, the Dallas Cowboys defeated the Baltimore Ravens 27-17, largely due to the stellar performance of their new star quarterback, Dak Prescott. As an SEC football fan, I had been watching this young man develop as a leader and athlete during his legendary collegiate career at Mississippi State University. He took the Bulldogs to a level of play I hadn't seen them exhibit in my lifetime. Prescott left college to play in the NFL with records, wins, and a reputation as an athlete to watch. When the Cowboys took the field that night, the fans in Dallas were already taking a fun ride on the Dak bandwagon. He was lighting up the NFL with a rookie season that shattered all the expectations of the experts.

While this night produced yet another win to add to Prescott's resume, it would be a seemingly insignificant event that took place on the sideline that would tell the world more about this talented athlete than his playmaking in the game.

As he stood on the sideline, Prescott took a drink of water from a paper cup, crumpled it into a ball, and tossed it in the direction of a nearby trashcan. He missed. That's right, the star quarterback for America's football team couldn't hit a trashcan with a cup! OK, so he's not Michael Jordan. But it's what happened next that would dominate sports news headlines for the next week. Dak Prescott, star quarterback, walked over to pick up the cup and threw it in the trash. Now, he could have, like so many other guys in his shoes would have done, just left it for one of the many sideline assistants to handle. After all, he had a game to play. He's an important guy with an important job. But on this night, Prescott made a decision to go above and beyond when he had no idea the world was watching.

Colin Cowherd, one of the top sports news personalities in the nation, summed it up well the next morning on national radio and television when he said, "Little things always become big things."[1]

At first glance, Prescott's simple act may seem insignificant. But when you understand the principle behind it, that moment on the sideline takes on great meaning. According to Cowherd, an athlete who will do the seemingly small things like Prescott did that day will also give a coach one more rep in a workout and one more burst of effort to win a game.[2] You see, what the world saw when Prescott thought no one was watching, revealed the admirable character inside this young man. A person who understands the importance of doing the little things well, can also be counted on to handle the big things.

We see the "little things become big things" principle at work in the life of King Saul. In his case, we'll learn how detrimental it can be to neglect the little things, especially when it comes to the issues of our hearts.

A survey of the landscape of King Saul's story reveals small cracks in the foundation of his character that will eventually lead to a broken life, a broken family, and a crumbling kingdom.

He can't seem to trust God's call on his life, so he hides in fear. He loves the power the crown gives him, but never accepts the responsibility it demands. He struggles with fully obeying God's instructions. His insecurities cause him to distrust those who are loyal to him, while his arrogance will cause him to assume roles he was never given. His intense desire for the approval of people leads him to despise anyone who receives praise other than himself. Saul's anger issues seem advantageous in early battles but eventually erupt like a volcano spewing lava-like consequences across his home and kingdom.

We watch Saul's life and reign for decades as he continues to allow his issues to go unchecked year after year. Through his story, we see clearly that our issues don't remain dormant if we choose to ignore them, but instead pick up steam like a locomotive moving down the tracks. And, just like an out of control train, Saul's sin will end up destroying anyone and anything in his path. His family, his friends, his supporters, and his subjects will all be impacted.

But while Saul walked a thousand miles away from God's plan for his life, God was always waiting for him to take one step back into His grace. Years of mistakes also included years of opportunities for repentance that could have saved Saul's life. But, instead of turning to God, Saul continued to trivialize and make excuses for his sin.

This isn't just Saul's story—it's our story. It's the story of humanity's struggle since the beginning of time.

[MALIGNANT MINIMIZATION]

For all have sinned and fall short of the glory of God. (Romans 3:23 ESV)

As humans, we have an innate tendency to minimize our sin. When an area of sin is exposed in our life, our instinctive reaction is almost always to try to hide it or make excuses. We try to deflect and are tempted to point a finger in someone else's direction either in blame or comparison. We comfort ourselves in our dysfunction with thoughts like, "Hey, I may not be perfect, but at least I'm not as bad as some other people I know." We get defensive or we downplay it.

Whatever the case may be, the danger in refusing to own up to our sin is that it keeps us from repentant transformation. And, just like a person who notices the unmistakable signs of disease in their body but ignores them, the result is a metastasizing of our issues that, if not treated, will destroy us.

At the root of Saul's unwillingness to confront his sin—and our own ambivalence toward our issues—is a basic misunderstanding of the nature of sin.

In defining "sin" in the book of Romans, the apostle Paul uses an archery term that means "to miss the mark" of God's perfect standard.[3] And we're all guilty of missing that target. But while we tend to think of our sin primarily in terms of our actions, the reality of our sin condition is deeper than what we do or don't do—or how close we think we can get to the target.

While the Bible is clear that our individual actions carry varying degrees of earthly consequences, *all sin* is a form of rebellion against God and subject to His fully justified wrath and judgment against it.

I know that's heavy but stay with me.

Humanity's problem could not be solved simply with behavior modification—the law showed us that. The Bible drops the full weight of this reality in the book of James.

> *For whoever keeps the whole law and yet stumbles at just one point is guilty of breaking all of it. (James 2:10 NIV)*

To truly understand these words is to feel the walls of

our sin reality close in on us with an inescapable truth—there is nothing we could do to attain God's standard of holiness. But this, after all, is the function of the law in our lives.

> *Therefore no one will be declared righteous in God's sight by the works of the law; rather, through the law we become conscious of our sin. (Romans 3:20 NIV)*

The law could never save us, but its purpose was to reveal our inability to save ourselves and send us running into the arms of a gracious and loving God who could. God used the law as a spotlight to expose the darkness in our soul and the hopelessness of our situation—not to shame us, but to show us our need for a Savior.

Here is where we often run into problems. So many times, we allow the shame we feel over our sin to create distance between our hearts and God. Just like Adam and Eve, we think we can hide and handle the problem ourselves. Instead of turning to God when they ate from the forbidden tree in the garden, Adam and Eve hid from Him and used fig leaves to cover themselves in a futile attempt at self-salvation.

And we have our own modern-day fig leaves, too. We try to cover up an unhealthy family with a beautiful home. We use misleading social media posts to cover our unfulfilled and empty lives. We use money to mask our pain and busyness to hide our boredom. And while these "fig leaves" will *never* succeed in covering our brokenness, they will *always* hinder us from experiencing the healing and wholeness God longs to give us.

Here's the thing—if we view our sin as a small enough issue that we think we can take care of it ourselves, we're deceived about our situation and we've completely missed the point of the Gospel.

Jesus ran into this deadly self-righteousness with the religious leaders of His day. The Pharisees prided themselves in their ability to keep the law. They viewed themselves as superior to the "sinners" Jesus chose to spend His time with.

In Mark 2:17, Jesus told the Pharisees that He had not come for the healthy but for the sick—not for those who *thought* they were righteous but for those who *knew* they were sinners. By believing they were spiritually well because of their religious performance, the Pharisees disqualified themselves from receiving His help.

Jesus blew up the notion that keeping the law could ever save humanity and went straight to the heart of the matter with his famous and brilliant Sermon on the Mount.[4] He said that murder and anger, adultery and lustful thoughts, were all subject to the same judgment (different earthly consequences but identical heart implications). It's only when we view the nature of our sin in this way—the same way God views it—that true repentance and heart transformation can take place in our lives.

King Saul never saw his sin the same way God did. He had a habit of malignant minimization regarding his sin that kept him mired in destructive rebellion. What if he'd taken his weaknesses seriously early on and fallen to his knees in humble submission to his faithful God? What difference would it have made in his life and in the lives of those who loved him? Rather than minimizing his sin, Saul could have minimized the damage incurred because of it.

What about us? Are there issues in our life that seem to be under control right now, but if left unchecked, have the potential to cause major problems down the road?

A boat sailing across an ocean at a mere degree off course will over time end up thousands of miles from its intended destination. Remember, the little things become the big things.

Are we ignoring our blind spots or allowing God to illuminate our errant path by His truth to keep us from veering too far off course in our own life's journey?

Chapter Three
The Wrong Fear Choice

[1] There was a man of Benjamin whose name was Kish, the son of Abiel, son of Zeror, son of Becorath, son of Aphiah, a Benjaminite, a man of wealth. [2] And he had a son whose name was Saul, a handsome young man. There was not a man among the people of Israel more handsome than he. From his shoulders upward he was taller than any of the people. (1 Samuel 9:1-2 ESV)

[THE MASK]

Growing up in the '80s, my childhood view of masculinity was largely influenced by the action-adventure movies and TV shows of the decade. Iconic figures like Hulk Hogan and Macho Man, Rambo and Rocky Balboa, and GI Joe and the Masters of the Universe all had an impact on my perception of "manhood" as a kid. But, my favorite Hollywood hero of the era was the private investigator, Thomas Sullivan Magnum. Every week, my eyes were glued to the next high-octane, action-packed episode of *Magnum, P.I.* With a mean set of skills to beat the bad guys, posh beachfront living in Hawaii, a red Ferrari, and killer good looks (you're welcome, Tom Selleck), Magnum seemed to be the total package.

Saul, son of Kish and the tribe of Benjamin, looked like the total package, too. He was the Magnum of his day. There are only a few times in Scripture where we're told that a person is handsome, and one of those times is in reference to Saul. The Bible tells us Saul was the most handsome man in the nation of Israel, with an impressive stature that made him stand out in any crowd. His family background was replete with honor and wealth. He looked the part, and he had the pedigree.

When it came to a trophy king, Israel definitely had its man.

But as the saying goes, "looks can be deceiving." Over time I've learned clichés become clichés for a reason—they tend to be true. What we find under King Saul's regal exterior is a deeply flawed core full of unresolved character issues waiting to surface.

[THE CORE]

You shall solemnly forewarn them, and show them the behavior of the king who will reign over them. (1 Samuel 8:9 NKJV)

The truth is we all have a core, or an inner man, buried beneath whatever mask we show to the world.

Some of us, like Saul, are able to hide a great deal and do it really well. Others have a more difficult time keeping the cracked façade from leaking.

The bodybuilder who has the physical strength to bench 300 pounds but is too weak to commit to a relationship. The CEO who runs her company with confidence but lacks the courage to end a toxic friendship. The student who boasts of a perfect GPA but who cuts corners and even cheats to make the grade.

The biggest problem with masking our weaknesses is that as long as we keep them covered up, we will never be able to confront and overcome them. Saul may have been able to hide his weaknesses up until this point in his life, but the pressure from the crown being placed on him now was about to reveal what had been lying dormant all along.

To be clear, God ultimately chose Saul to be Israel's first king. And, from the vantage point of history, we can now see that He, as always, had a perfect long-term plan. However, this doesn't diminish the fact that Saul was chosen *at the request of the people,* not in accordance with the way God intended for His people to be ruled.

You see, sometimes God allows us to have what we think we want, to show us that what we really need is Him. God lovingly instructed Samuel to tell the Israelites the harsh truth about their future king, but they refused to listen. The deception of their hearts spoke louder than the truth. Israel is getting the leader it deserves at this point in its history.

They asked for an earthly king, and God is giving them one.

The first of Saul's issues comes to light at his coronation. As strong and impressive as Saul was, he wrestled with fear—the wrong kind of fear.

[THE CORONATION]

But when they sought him he could not be found. [22]*So they inquired again of the Lord, "Is there a man still to come?" and the Lord said, "Behold, he has hidden himself among the baggage."* (1Samuel 10:22 ESV)

When it came time to publicly coronate Saul as King of Israel, they couldn't find him. It must have been frustrating to finally get to that highly-anticipated moment only to find that the star attraction has gone AWOL. The band is playing, the people are chanting his name, the shiny crown awaits with all of its splendor and power, yet Saul is doing what we do so many times when fearful of stepping into what God has asked us to do—he's hiding. Like a wild animal alluding a pack of track dogs, Saul tries to escape the weight of responsibility and expectations about to overtake him.

Rather than embracing the holy fear of the One who had called him and had promised to be with him, Saul let the fear of the people and the position send him running from his future.

This holy fear, or what Scripture refers to as "the fear of the Lord," is a respect and reverence of Him that leads to worship and obedience. It's a fear that drives us into the arms of a loving God rather than away from Him. The Bible teaches that "the fear of the Lord is the beginning of all wisdom."[1] It leads to blessing, honor, and life.[2] It's the fear that can dispel all other fears—the fear of man, the fear of failure, fear of the future, even fear of death itself.

Proverbs 14:26 says that "in the fear of the Lord there is strong confidence." It's a firm foundation of trust on which we can build our life.

But as Saul looked at his future, he wasn't so confident. The reason Saul feared stepping into God's call for his life publicly was that he had failed to listen when God confirmed this call to him privately.

[THE CONFIRMATION]

Then Samuel took a flask of oil and poured it on his head and kissed him and said, "Has not the Lord appointed you to be prince over His people Israel? And you shall reign over the people of the Lord and you will save them from the hand of their surrounding enemies. And this shall be the sign to you that the Lord has anointed you to be prince over His heritage." (1 Samuel 10:1 ESV)

Taking things public without solidifying them

privately often leads to disaster. Throwing your son on a pitcher's mound in front of his peers without working with him on the fundamentals first can lead to embarrassment that he'll carry for a long time. Failing to practice your speech before standing up to give the presentation may lead to a communication fiasco from which it's hard to recover.

God is always preparing us along the way for what He has prepared for us in the future.

You see, Saul's first brush with his call to be a king wasn't at his public coronation, but at a dramatic private confirmation. When Saul first arrives on the scene in Scripture, we find him three days into a search for his father's lost donkeys. At the suggestion of his servant, he goes into the city to find the prophet, hoping that Samuel can provide guidance on the whereabouts of the donkeys. Needless to say, he comes away from that divine appointment with more than he ever expected.

God not only led Samuel to anoint Saul with oil, which signified that he was chosen by the Lord, but He kindly gave Saul three unmistakable signs for his journey home to bolster his confidence.

First, Samuel told Saul that two men would meet him with news that his father's donkeys had been found. Secondly, a little farther down the road, he would encounter three men—one carrying three young goats, another carrying three loaves of bread, and another carrying a skin of wine. Again, the signs were unique, personal, and unmistakable.

Finally, Samuel told Saul that he would meet a procession of prophets and instrumentalists worshiping

God. The Spirit of the Lord would come upon him, and he would prophesy with them and be turned into a different man.

God would empower and equip Saul with everything he needed for his calling—and He promises to do the same for you and me.

All of the signs prophesied by Samuel came to pass. It's evident that God gave Saul every reason to trust Him and step into his potential with confidence. But Saul refused to believe that God was sufficient. Instead of resting in His power, Saul would perpetually seek to do things by his own strength.

[THE CHOICE]

For God gave us a spirit not of fear but of power and love and self-control. (2 Timothy 1:7 ESV)

Like many of us at times, Saul chose the wrong fear. Had Saul determined in his heart to fear the Lord above all else, he would have trusted in His promises and His plan. But Saul would never fully trust God, and the fear that ruled Saul's life would cause him to make destructive choices throughout his reign.

Like Saul, we have to decide which fear to choose. *Fear God or fear people? Fear God or fear our current situation? Fear God or fear the future?*

The most repeated command in Scripture is "do not fear." The Bible tells us that fear is not from God. When we choose to reject the wrong fear, a great exchange takes place. We trade our weakness for power, insecurity for love, and foolishness for self-control. We step into a source of strength that will sustain us and enable us to fulfill God's plan and purpose for our life.

As Saul stood shaking in his sandals and hiding from his future, God could see him. God could see who Saul could become but knew with sovereign foreknowledge that he never would. He could see the outward kingly exterior but also the inner turmoil.

This same God sees us as well. He sees the fear we battle internally. He sees us standing at the edge of our future like a child with toes curled around the end of a diving board afraid to take the plunge into the adventure of God that awaits. Will we choose to turn back in fear or jump in with holy confidence, trusting in the God who keeps His promises?

Ready or not, Saul was about to be thrust into the deep end.

Then they ran and took him from there. (1 Samuel 10:23 ESV)

Saul's time had come, and God had given him everything he needed for this moment. Sadly, Saul would accept the crown that day, but refuse to allow God to mold him into a man worthy to truly wear it. Saul would forfeit his future to fear and eventually break the crown that was chosen for him.

Chapter Four
Impaired Condition

In the northwestern part of Washington state, there's a picturesque part of the Puget Sound known as the Tacoma Narrows Strait that separates the Kitsap Peninsula from the city of Tacoma. The area is not only beautiful but extremely windy, with gusts sometimes reaching 30-40 miles per hour whipping the water into what looks like a frothy boil.

It's these blustery conditions that led to the infamous collapse of the first Tacoma Narrows Bridge in 1940.

As the population of the area grew, so did the need for a bridge that would connect the two sides of the strait. In September of 1938, construction began on what would be the third-longest suspension bridge in the world at the time. Because traffic across the sound was thought to be light, the bridge was built relatively narrow and shallow compared to its length—a decision that would prove to be lethal to its performance.

On November 7, 1940, just four months after its

completion, a strong wind gust caused the bridge to twist violently to its breaking point and collapse into the white-capped water below.[1]

The word "integrity" is used in a number of different ways and contexts, but it's very applicable in the arena of engineering and construction. Webster's Dictionary defines integrity as "an unimpaired condition."

When the strong Tacoma winds came barreling through the strait that day, it became clear the Tacoma Narrows Bridge lacked structural integrity. It was, in fact, very much impaired.

Vintage film footage of the event looks like a scene scripted in Hollywood, but it was all too real. A local newspaper editor and his dog were the last to attempt to drive on the bridge. In the terrifying moments of the wind-induced upheaval, the man barely escaped his car as he ran for his life amidst the explosive sound of cracking concrete. Eventually, he had to crawl on bruised and bloodied knees for 500 yards to get to the safety of solid ground.[2] He and some stunned onlookers watched as the bridge plummeted into the deep waters of the Puget Sound.

> So Saul said, "Bring a burnt offering and peace offerings here to me." And he offered the burnt offering. (1 Samuel 13:9 NKJV)

King Saul's second year on the throne was barely behind him when the winds of testing began to blow against his character. Like the Washington bridge, this test would not end well.

A battle was brewing with Israel's most dangerous enemy. The Philistines were legendary warriors with a total disdain for Israel and their God. Their army was massive, well-trained and fully-equipped for effective ancient warfare. The Israelites were understandably nervous as they looked to Saul for leadership.

The prophet Samuel, the only man with the authority to make official sacrifices to God, instructed Saul to wait for him to arrive and make these crucial offerings to God. It was the custom to take part in this beautiful ceremony that signified trust and dependence upon the Living God before going to battle. Saul, under pressure from the people, just could not wait. He disobediently offers the sacrifice himself, breaking God's commands and revealing a character flaw that will eventually bring his life and kingdom to the breaking point. The man wearing Israel's crown was living with an impaired condition.

And Samuel said, "What have you done?" (1 Samuel 13:11 NKJV)

These four words from the mouth of the prophet would ring in Saul's royal ears the rest of his life.

We've all been there, haven't we? We've made decisions in a moment that had a much greater impact than we could have imagined. We've spouted words in anger that we'd give anything to be able to take back.

Like Saul's unlawful sacrifices, some things can't be undone. Some decisions end up changing everything.

If you're like me, you've been the one asking yourself *what have I done?* So often in my life, I've been completely dismayed by my own actions. Looking back, I wonder incredulously how I could have been so unwise and blind to the obvious implications of my poor choices. Like a boomerang thrown from the hand and then returning with even greater force, our decisions often come back with more consequence than we ever expected.

But just like in the case of King Saul, there's a path that can be traced that led us to our key moments of failure. Every bridge that fails had a defective design behind it. Every bad decision made was a result of a wrong thought pattern. Both the Tacoma Narrows Bridge and the leadership of King Saul had faulty blueprints.

[BLUEPRINT FOR FAILURE]

> *Saul said, "When I saw that the people were scattered from me, and that you did not come within the days appointed, and that the Philistines gathered together at Michmash, then I said, 'the Philistines will now come down on me at Gilgal, and I have not made supplication to the Lord.' Therefore I felt compelled and offered the burnt offering."*
> *(1 Samuel 13:11-12 NKJV)*

In the aftermath of the Tacoma Narrows Bridge

disaster, it became evident that the design of the bridge was defective from the beginning. In fact, the designers and builders knew this and had tried to fix the problem to no avail. During the construction process, the bridge would sway in the wind so much that it earned the nickname "Galloping Gertie."

The powerful winds that rushed in that day didn't *create* the lack of integrity in the bridge—they *revealed* it.

That's how integrity works. When the pressure of life inevitably comes, it squeezes us like a sponge and forces out whatever is on the inside. It reveals the true nature of our heart's condition—either strong or impaired.

King Saul's life-changing mistake was a product of an underlying problem that had been lurking beneath the surface from the start. Saul had a problem with insecurity that was rooted in an identity crisis.

Remember where we found Saul just before his coronation? He was hiding. He was afraid and unsure of his ability to lead the nation. There's a small but telling detail the Scripture gives right after Saul is presented to the people. It says the crowd cheered for their new king—all but a few.

> But some worthless fellows said, "How can this man save us?" And they despised him and brought him no present. But he held his peace. (1 Samuel 10:27 ESV)

Do you see it? Hundreds of thousands of people heaped their adoration on Saul, but he noticed the handful who didn't. The newly-formed crown was barely warm on his head, but the blueprint for an identity crisis was already there.

I can see Saul in the mirror of my own life. As a pastor, I get hundreds of emails each week from people to let me know how much they were encouraged by one of my sermons. But it's that one negative email that I remember—the one I allow to drain my energy and self-confidence. I'm often amazed at my inability to ignore some of the very same things that were a distraction for Saul, too.

You see, Saul wasn't convinced of his identity—his God-given identity—so he looked to outside sources to affirm it. I bet you sometimes do the same. I know I do.

If we're not convinced of who God says we are, we'll make unwise and potentially destructive decisions in the search for our identity. Because King Saul had never fully found his secure identity in the God who chose and confirmed him, he sought the praise of the people. His appetite for their approval caused him to disobey God and make an offering he was forbidden to make.

Saul's desire to be affirmed by the people rather than approved by God would cause a massive breach of leadership integrity for the throne of Israel.

Our identity issues are heart strings that our spiritual enemy loves to play. It leads young singles to lay aside their purity in search of love. It drives pastors to compare their ministries with others, turning a holy calling into a competitive game. It causes a person to tear down another in an effort to make themselves look better. It keeps us from living the life of fulfillment, purpose, and peace we were designed to live.

As His children, God has given us our true identity. When we grasp who our Creator says that we are, we're no longer compelled to live from a place of insecurity and are empowered to live a life of integrity.

In a sense, integrity means *strength*. It means that something or someone can be trusted to stand. A bridge with structural integrity has the strength to safely hold the assigned weight. A leader with integrity has the fortitude to make the tough decisions for the right reasons. And when the pressure of life weighs heavy on you and me, it's the strength found in our God-given identity that will enable us to walk in integrity.

Throughout Scripture, God always strengthened those He used greatly by clarifying their identity.

- *Abram the wanderer becomes Abraham the father of the faith.*
- *Jacob the deceiver becomes Israel the chosen.*
- *Moses the exiled shepherd becomes Moses the legendary deliverer.*
- *Gideon the humble farmer becomes Israel's heroic warrior.*
- *Simon the fisherman becomes Peter the apostle and prominent leader of the early church.*
- *Saul the persecutor is transformed into Paul the fearless pastor.*

Even before Jesus begins His world-changing earthly ministry, the Father thunders a reminder of His identity as heaven's Son for all to hear.

Integrity is strength, and strength is found in a rock-solid identity given to us by God.

> *Yet to all who did receive him, to those who believed in his name, he gave the right to become children of God. (John 1:12 NIV)*

I grew up in a small home less than a mile from my grandparents' house. After school and most weekends, I would spend my time working with my Pop and playing in the woods around their home. In the evenings, I would meander down the dusty gravel road back home to parents who loved and cared deeply for me.

I loved this rural spot on the map because there was nowhere on the planet where I felt more secure. *I was confident in who I was because my parents and grandparents told me who I was.* I was a Bell. That name came with expectations: get up early and work hard, don't waste things, love one another and respect authority, love Jesus and His church, read the Bible. These were integral parts of the formation of my identity. But most of all, my family made certain I knew that I was loved unconditionally. I was a son. I was a grandson. I *mattered* on that little dirt road in Mississippi, and that gave me strength. It's that strength that helped me build a life of integrity. And *that* is the power of knowing who you are.

God tried to tell Saul who he was, but he refused to listen. This sent him on a search for his identity down the darkest of roads.

God has told us who we are as well. Are we listening?

The Gospel of John tells us that through Jesus, we have been made children of God. We've been adopted into His family, and it was the most expensive adoption of all time. It cost Jesus His life. As sons and daughters of God, we've been made secure for eternity and are empowered to live a life free from insecurity here and now.

Not only are we His children, but Scripture also tells us that we're friends of God.[3] It's unimaginable that former rebels of God would now be called His companions, but that's the beautiful reality of who we are.

As followers of Christ, we're invited to step into a life of purpose that Scripture says was planned for us before the foundations of the earth were created. Our life now has great significance as we're called to come alongside Him to build His Kingdom on the earth.

When the truth that we are completely accepted and unconditionally loved by our Father penetrates our hearts, it will transform our lives. We no longer have to perform for the approval of people because we've been fully approved by God through Jesus. We no longer have to live enslaved by the opinions of others because of the freedom of knowing who we are in Christ.

Son. Daughter. Friend. Chosen. Masterpiece. That's what the Creator of the Universe says about us.

This reality also changes how we view our obedience to God. You see, if we're just focused on following the rules, we will eventually face a temptation that our rulebook can't fight. But when we have a fire of affection burning in our heart for our Father, we genuinely desire to please Him. His law becomes our delight when we are fully confident in God's love for us. Integrity isn't the ability to keep the rules. That's simply not possible for us. Integrity is a strength graciously *given* to us. A life of integrity is built from the blueprint of our God-given identity made possible in Christ.

> ¹³*And Samuel said to Saul, "You have done foolishly. You have not kept the command of the Lord your God, with which he commanded you. For then the Lord would have established your kingdom over Israel forever.* ¹⁴ *But now your kingdom shall not continue. The Lord has sought out a man after his own heart, and the Lord has commanded him to be prince over his people, because you have not kept what the Lord commanded you." (1 Samuel 13:13-14 ESV)*

Samuel tells Saul the painful truth—he could have been an amazing king. God would have blessed Saul's reign and established his kingdom had Saul only trusted Him enough to obey. But Saul never rested in the security of God's love for him. He never truly understood what it meant to be God's child.

How much pain have we all endured as a result of our disobedience? A life of integrity won't be built simply on our ability to be good rule followers. Integrity is the result of obedience born out of our love for God. The reality is, Saul disobeyed God because he *wanted* to. Saul lost his love for God's law because he no longer delighted in God Himself. Saul's insecurity and disobedience cost him the crown and his kingdom.

What about in our own lives? How much will we lose because of our identity crisis? How will those around us suffer because of our refusal to be who God created and called us to be?

One of the greatest gifts God gives us in Christ is a new identity. One of the greatest gifts we can give ourselves and those around us is to live confidently in that identity.

In choosing to disobey God and offer the sacrifice, Saul would ultimately sacrifice his crown. God saw that Saul's heart lacked the integrity needed to hold the weight of leadership Israel needed. God's hand of blessing and favor that Saul had enjoyed was lifted from his life. God never stopped loving Saul and he didn't cease to be God's child. But, like a runaway, Saul could never fully experience the love and blessing of his Father. This will impact the rest of his life and reign and keep his heart in a perpetual "impaired condition." His insecurity will lead him to continue to break God's law. It will cause him to see loyal friends as despised enemies and to view blessings as curses. Insecurity always fogs up the lenses of our lives. It's in finding our security in Christ alone that we're given clarity, and that clarity paves the way to integrity.

Chapter Five
The Pride of Partial Obedience

One Christmas, we bought my kids a new basketball goal. My plan was to put the goal together after we put the kids to sleep on Christmas Eve. Perfect plan. But, as I was unloading the parts from the box, to my dismay, the parts just kept coming. It looked as if they took a perfectly simple basketball goal, tore it into a million pieces, and then simply chunked it into a big box. One of my dear friends from church happened to call me at this moment, and when I told him what I was up to, he laughed. He'd been through the same ordeal himself before and offered to help me.

Historically, when males put something together, the general rule is that the instruction manual will be considered only when absolutely necessary. The goal is to get the job done with as little manufacturer input as possible. We were two-thirds of the way into completing the multi-step project when things came to a screeching halt. We thought that we'd generally followed the instructions, but what we failed to realize was that an intricate project with hundreds of parts requires precision, taking the correct steps at the correct time. Sequence matters. Parts matter. General adherence to the manual wasn't working. We learned that obedience to instructions matters. My friend and I were forced to frustratingly take the goal apart piece by piece to get back to the point where we got off the plan. It was only a few steps that we had missed, but to not follow all the instructions in this instance was to not follow them at all.

King Saul had a big problem with instruction manuals. In truth, he had a problem with authority in his life altogether. Although he had already made a crucial mistake by making an offering that he was forbidden to make in the biblical instruction, God gives Saul a chance to write a new story later. God commands Saul to lead the army into battle with the formidable Amalekites. Not only does He want Saul to defeat this army, He wants him to completely destroy the entire group of people along with their belongings and property.

Here's the thing about obedience to God's commands: sometimes they don't make sense. Saul surely wondered why he needed to obliterate this group of people. Consistent obedience to God's commands often requires a trust in His understanding and purposes that goes beyond our ability to comprehend. Sometimes we simply must obey whether we get it or not. We can be sure God always has his reasons, and they are always good reasons.

In Saul's case, he chose to partially obey God, which led to a final nail in the coffin of his sad story. His life will go on, and he'll keep wearing the crown, but he will not have God's blessing, which was the greatest loss of all.

> [2]*Thus says the Lord of Hosts, "I have noted what Amalek did to Israel in opposing them on the way when they came out of Egypt.* [3]*Now go and strike Amalek and devote to destruction all that they have."* (1 Samuel 15:2-3 ESV)

God is clear. Saul is to battle the Amalekites and totally destroy everything connected to them. This was a nation who hated God and was raising generation after generation to hate Him and His people. He wanted the property destroyed because it was crucial that Israel know they did not need the plunder of godless nations to survive. Their God could handle that just fine. God knew what He was doing, and Saul was the man He wanted to do it through.

> [17]*Remember what Amalek did to you on the way as you came out of Egypt,* [18]*how he attacked you on the way when you were faint and weary, and cut off your tail, those who were lagging behind you, and he did not fear God.* (Deuteronomy 25:17-18 ESV)

To see God's reasons for this aggressive command,

we must turn the ancient pages of Israel's history backwards. When the people of God were in the middle of the famed Exodus from Egypt, the Amalekites were not helpful to them and even attacked them where they were most vulnerable. They did not respect the Living God of the Israelites, and they were also cowardly in the way they attacked. Instead of attacking them bravely in open battle, they met Israel in the back of the line, where the women, children, sick, and elderly would have been. This was ancient terrorism, and God would not forget it.

Even though Saul had blown it earlier in his reign, God was giving him another chance. He was choosing to use Saul to accomplish His purpose in avenging the Amalekite attack on the Israelites years later. This is an example of God's unbelievable grace in our lives. I could tell you many stories of God giving me chances to write better stories with my life even after I've failed miserably. I bet you have the same story. God loves telling beautiful stories with imperfect people. He loves bringing strength out of brokenness. This is the God who took Joseph from a desert pit to an Egyptian palace. He brought Moses from obscurity to world renowned leadership. He would one day take David from sinful despair to blessed restoration. He can do the same for you and me. He wanted to do the same for Saul.

⁷And Saul defeated the Amalekites from Havilah as far as Shur, which is east of Egypt. ⁸And he took Agag the king of the Amalekites alive and devoted to destruction all the people with the edge of the sword. ⁹But Saul and the people spared Agag and the best of the sheep and of the oxen and of the fattened calves and the lambs, and all that was good, and would not utterly destroy them. All that was despised and worthless they devoted to destruction. ¹⁰The word of the Lord came to Samuel: ¹¹"I regret that I have made Saul king, for he has turned back from following me and has not performed my commandments." And Samuel was angry, and he cried to the Lord all night. (1 Samuel 15:7-11 ESV)

The story starts so well. Saul was always a good warrior, so it's no surprise the Amalekites were no match for him and his army. Starting well was Saul's way. His kingdom started well. Remember, in his first year as king, Saul was being used and empowered mightily by the Spirit of God to do great things. On this day, Saul's beginning will be victorious, but he will be unable to finish strong. He obeys God magnificently only to stop halfway to the finish line.

The truth of the matter is, Saul kept the king alive and the good possessions of the Amalekites because he *wanted* to. He decided that his desire was more important than God's commands, and when anyone makes this decision, it is a form of rebellion. God's command just didn't make sense to Saul, so he made some changes to the plan. Surely God would understand. Why waste good stuff? Why destroy things the Israelites could use?

Saul was simply displaying his love for Israel and his immense wisdom, right? Not a chance. Saul was displaying his pride. He believed he knew better than God. The foundation of all disobedience, and all partial obedience, is pride.

> [13]*Then Samuel went to Saul, and Saul said to him, "Blessed are you of the Lord! I have performed the commandment of the Lord."* [14]*But Samuel said, "What then is this bleating of the sheep in my ears, and the lowing of the oxen which I hear?"* (1 Samuel 15:13-14 NKJV)

One could literally hear Saul's disobedience. It couldn't be hidden. His blatant rebellion was walking around in plain sight. Amazingly, Saul believes he has obeyed the Lord. That's how pride works. It is always visible to observers before it is visible to the one who is prideful. Imagine the power of the prophet's words as he called Saul on the carpet. *What then is this? If you've obeyed, Saul, why are there still sheep? Why is this king alive?* Saul had been deceived by his own pride.

> *God resists the proud, but gives grace to the humble.* (1 Peter 5:5 NKJV)

When a tsunami crashes onto the shore, it's only natural to focus on the moment of impact and the devastation that follows. But what often goes undetected is the actual source of the destruction. Somewhere far beneath the waterline miles away from shore, the earth's tectonic plates have shifted. The water displaced by the shift generates a huge pulse of energy that picks up speed and maintains its strength as it travels across the ocean.[1] What the world sees when the massive wave hits the shore in reality began long before impact.

The wave of Saul's pride had been building for years. It started small—a decision here, a thought there, a shortcut here, a rebellious action there.

When the ink was beginning to flow on a story of restoration for Saul, he pridefully snatched the pen into his own hand and wrote his own story. It doesn't end well. Saul again and again argues to Samuel that he did obey God. Samuel is unmoved. There will be no talking his way out of this.

> [22]*So Samuel said: "Has the Lord as great delight in burnt offerings and sacrifices, As in obeying the voice of the Lord? Behold, to obey is better than sacrifice, And to heed than the fat of rams.* [23]*For rebellion is as the sin of witchcraft, And stubbornness is as iniquity and idolatry. Because you have rejected the word of the Lord, He also has rejected you from being king." (1 Samuel 15:22-23 NKJV)*

God was looking for obedience from Saul, and He's looking for obedience from us. When we obey, it means that we trust. Saul simply did not trust God and His commands.

When my kids were small, I would ask them to jump from our trampoline into my arms. They would just sail right off of that thing smiling ear to ear. Every time they jumped into my arms, they were proclaiming their trust in me. They trusted that I would catch them, and I wouldn't drop them. They trusted their dad, and that trust brought me great joy.

When we disobey God, we are displaying a lack of trust in Him. We distrust His wisdom, His understanding, and His goodness. Imagine the heart of the Father when we refuse to jump in obedience. Saul's distrust in God was displayed in his prideful disobedience. This grieved the heart of God, and it unleashed a torrent of consequences in Saul's life and kingdom.

Partial obedience is disobedience. Disobedience broke Saul's crown, and it will break our lives.

Chapter Six
Paying for Passivity

In the early 2000s, I was a youth minister in the metro-Atlanta area. I loved the opportunity God had given me to impact the lives of the teenagers and parents involved in our large suburban church. Most of the students were from wealthy families, and my wife and I would chuckle each week as we watched the parking lot of the church fill up with luxury cars belonging to high schoolers with no jobs but very rich parents. When it came to the latest and the greatest money could buy, these kids had it all.

One Sunday after service, the father of one of the students approached me to discuss an issue he'd been having with his daughter. He invited me to their home to discuss possible solutions to the gridlock situation he was experiencing with her. He seemed genuine in his concern, and I felt honored to be able to help.

When my wife and I arrived at the stunning estate,

we were escorted into the living area and greeted by a roaring fireplace and coffee table full of hors d'oeuvres. This house was beautiful.

But hiding beneath the storybook veneer was a toxic family setting where a leadership vacuum had created a relational minefield.

We talked with the father for half an hour about the myriad issues with which this teenage girl was dealing. She had seemingly gone from an outgoing kid with lots of friends and activities to a sullen loner who wanted to do nothing but retreat to her bedroom.

She had refused to come downstairs, so my wife and I asked if we could go up to her room and try to get her to open up about what was wrong. We talked and prayed for her as she just sat glaring back at us. As we turned to go downstairs, I could sense there was a missing piece to this puzzle. I pressed the father for a little more information and found that the daughter had recently struck up a friendship with an older woman in her mid-20s. This woman did not share the family's faith or foundational values and was a vocal critic of everything for which our church stood. The woman, he admitted, had gained significant influence over his daughter's life, and that much of the alone time in her bedroom was spent on the phone with this negative influencer.

The initial solution to the problem was so obvious to me I almost felt embarrassed to have to point it out to the gentleman. I mean, after all, I was a 24-year-old youth pastor giving counsel to an uber-successful businessman who was far more experienced than me in almost every way—almost.

You see, I was taught early on in my life that some battles *must* be fought. Sometimes the stakes are too high to risk sitting passively by hoping an issue will resolve itself.

I told the father he needed to instruct his daughter to stop communicating with this woman. If she refused to cut off the relationship, he should remove her phone from her room. He stared at me with a perplexed look on his face and then spoke words that sounded like a verbal flag of surrender. "Oh, Pastor Chris, that's my daughter's personal space. I can't violate her privacy and autonomy in that way. I'll have to find another solution."

I couldn't believe what I was hearing. This father was facing a battle to protect his daughter and the peace of his home. This battle had *his* name on it. But, like so many people, he refused to fight the battle standing right in front of him that he alone was meant to fight.

You see, this father was resistant to my advice because he mistakenly thought I was suggesting he fight *against* his daughter. Wrong. I was challenging him to fight *for* her—to fight for his family and for his home.

On the battlefield of our lives, there will be things we fight *against* and things we will fight *for*. Identifying both is critical to winning the war.

King Saul was faced with one of the most important battles of his life and for the future of his kingdom. The Philistines had been a hostile enemy of Israel for a long time and were once again looking for a fight.

When we pick back up in 1 Samuel, we find the two armies camped on opposing hillsides overlooking an ominous valley below. Picture it like a natural coliseum of sorts with an arena in the middle just waiting for a bloody duel. And that's exactly what the Philistines wanted.

In ancient times, it was common for two armies to choose a warrior from among them to represent their respective nation in a one-on-one battle to the death. These battles were understood to have national implications. The Philistines had demanded this single combat solution because they were confident in their champion, the mighty giant named Goliath.

> [8]He stood and shouted to the ranks of Israel, "Why have you come out to draw up for battle? Am I not a Philistine, and are you not servants of Saul? Choose a man for yourselves, and let him come down to me. [9]If he is able to fight with me and kill me, then we will be your servants. But if I prevail against him and kill him, then you shall be our servants and serve us." [10]And the Philistine said, "I defy the ranks of Israel this day. Give me a man, that we may fight together." [11]When Saul and all Israel heard these words of the Philistine, they were dismayed and greatly afraid. (1 Samuel 17:8-11 ESV)

It's at this point in the story that we usually swing the spotlight in young David's direction. He famously shows up with lunch for his brothers but ends up fighting and defeating the giant with a slingshot and a rock.

But let's take a closer look at how David ended up in that valley in the first place. You see, this was not David's battle. This young man should have never had to carry the future of Israel on his inexperienced shoulders. The honor of Israel should have been won by the blade of Saul's sword instead of the rock in David's sling. This was Saul's battle. Goliath was Saul's giant. This was Saul's responsibility as Israel's warrior king.

The process for choosing a man for the challenge was simple. Find the biggest, strongest and most skilled fighter and send him on the battlefield. Goliath was the clear choice for the Philistines, and Saul was the obvious choice for Israel. When the arrogant giant taunted Israel with his challenge, he practically called out Saul by name.

This battle had Saul's name on it, yet Saul did nothing.

For forty days the Philistine came forward and took his stand, morning and evening. (1 Samuel 17:16 ESV)

The battles we're meant to fight won't just go away. They're waiting for us when we wake up in the morning, and they call out to us as we fall asleep.

Forty days is a long time to sit back and do nothing. Forty days is a long time to listen to your enemy mock you and dare you to come out for the battle.

King Saul was awakened in his royal tent each

morning by the alarm clock of a degrading call from a vile enemy. Night after night, torchlight danced in the angry eyes of Goliath as he stood defiantly in the valley and called out to the mighty man of Israel for a fight. But one would never come. Saul hoped, like many of us do, that the giant would simply go away. Saul didn't realize that every day the giant's challenge went unanswered, his own ability to lead the nation diminished. As Goliath grew louder, Saul became weaker.

We all have battles to fight—battles with our names on them. Saul had one. The passive father in my church had one. As spouses, we must fight the battle *for* our marriages. As parents, we must fight *for* our children. As singles, we must fight *for* our purity. As leaders, we must fight *for* the future of those we influence.

In all of these arenas, we will have to wage war *against* the enemies that seek to destroy what God has entrusted us to protect. We must fight *against* selfishness and pride. We must fight *against* temptation. We must fight *against* negative influences in our home. We must fight *against* our weaknesses and sinful tendencies.

Saul should have fought *against* the threat of the Philistines and *for* the honor of Israel, but he would do neither.

The verse reveals that Saul was afraid of the Philistine threat. And, because he was the leader, his fear spread throughout the entire military camp. Leaders are always the thermostat in the environments they influence. Whether it's in a business, home, or church, it's the leader who sets the tone.

The Israelites wanted a king who could rule from the throne with wisdom and fight on the battlefield with valor. Saul spent forty long days ignoring this responsibility. It would take a boy with the stature of a kid but the heart of a lion to defeat this enemy. Saul's unwillingness to engage in battle opened the door for another man to take the mantle of leadership from him. Though Saul would keep the title and the crown for a long time, the moment the giant's dead body hit the dirt of that valley, a new man held the hearts of Israel in his hands.

As David stood in the valley with Goliath's head in his hand, Saul watched the stunning victory from the tent of his passivity and fear. This should have been Saul's moment, but that day would forever belong to David. Saul would never be the same.

We've all known someone who has faced the devastating diagnosis of cancer. In fighting this potentially deadly enemy, you have two options—treat the cancer or cut it out. The thing you simply cannot do is ignore the disease in hopes that it will go away, not if you want to live. The reality is, cancer grows. Refusing to fight this disease could have grave consequences.

It's the same with the battles we face in our lives. They require that we take action. They must be fought. The skirmish we refuse to engage today becomes the all-out war we may be forced to fight in the future. To sit back and do nothing is simply not a viable option. For the cancer patient to allow fear to keep them from pursuing treatment can be fatal. While surgery is painful, and chemotherapy can be brutal, the alternative is usually much worse.

Our life battles will involve risk, injury, and possible defeat, but defeat is all but guaranteed when we refuse to engage in the fight.

Will we stand and fight the battle or sit back and hope our enemies will retreat? What will we do as the taunts of our giants grow louder?

We all have battles we're called to fight. It may be a relational battle. It may be an addiction. It may be a fight for a forgotten dream. Whatever the nature of the battle you're facing, the price you will pay for passivity will be far greater than the cost of action. Those we're entrusted to lead are counting on us to fight. Our commitment to engage in the battle now is the key that will unlock the door of victory in our future.

Saul's abdication of his responsibility to fight for Israel served as a reminder to the people of the frailty of an earthly king. Human kings have human weaknesses. Only the one true King of Israel would be willing to face the ultimate battle—not only for Israel, but for the entire world. King Jesus didn't run away from the battle. His crown was made of thorns and, instead of sitting on a throne, he was hung on a cross in an epic battle for the souls of mankind. It was a dangerous mission. It would cause Him unimaginable pain. This battle would cost the King His life. This King, instead of protecting Himself, would sacrifice Himself for you and me. He would fight against the enemy of our souls. He would fight for our salvation and ultimately His own glory. Our battle had His name on it. And He fought.

Chapter Seven
The Anger Edge

A hot-tempered man stirs up strife, but he who is slow to anger quiets contention. (Proverbs 15:18 ESV)

Disobedience always brings consequences. Some are felt immediately, and others come slowly rolling in like waves from a distant storm.

The consequences of Saul's disobedience hit the shore of his life when a good-looking country boy showed up with some rocks and a sling. David still had the blood of a giant on his boot when the adoring crowds started singing his praises and building his legend. Saul's lack of leadership created a space for David to begin his ascent to the throne. As the young man's fame grew, so did Saul's fury.

Saul's anger will prove to be a destructive force for the rest of his life, but it hadn't always been that way. Saul had experienced how anger could serve as a force for good when it was aligned with God and His purposes.

[RIVERS AND PONDS]

I grew up in southern Mississippi surrounded by the rivers, swamps, and creeks along the Gulf Coast. It was a great environment for a boy who loved the adventure of exploring the outdoors, but it could be a potentially dangerous one. I spent hours during the summer jumping from a rope swing into the Escatawpa River where it wasn't uncommon to see water moccasins as big as your leg (not to mention mosquitoes the size of bottle caps).

I lived on my grandfather's 200-acre farm, which had a large catfish pond on the property. It was on a steamy Southern afternoon that the water I loved so much would teach me a lesson I'd never forget.

I had long thought that if I could get out to the middle of the pond instead of casting from the bank, I could catch bigger fish. As I paddled out to the middle of the pond in my inflatable one-man boat, I started to imagine what it was going to be like to catch "the big one." Sure enough, I cast a spinnerbait and after only a couple turns of the reel, I hooked on to a monster.

Without thinking, I stood up to reel in the fish and my glorified life raft shot out from under me. Because I was caught off guard, I didn't have time to hold my breath when I fell into the pond, and I swallowed way too much water.

Now, this wouldn't have been a problem had it happened on the river. You see, rivers are exponentially cleaner because the water is *moving*. There's a continuous filtering that takes place as the water flows over rocks and through vegetation.

Ponds are a different story. Pond water doesn't move. A pond acts as nature's petri dish that, while creating an environment where fish can thrive, also becomes a breeding ground for bacteria and disease. In short, you don't want to drink the pond water. It took a round of antibiotics to get my stomach back on track after that fishing incident.

In our lives, anger works a lot like water. Let's be honest, we all get angry. It's a natural human emotion. In fact, Jesus got angry and God expresses anger in the Bible. The emotion of anger is not sinful. But anger, just like water, if left to remain stagnate, will become toxic.

Be angry and do not sin; do not let the sun go down on your anger. (Ephesians 4:26 ESV)

The first half of this verse in Ephesians tells us that anger is a natural part of the human experience and that's okay. The second part of the verse commands us to not let the day end without dealing with our anger. Our anger cannot be left to sit and stew but must be forced to *move* in a positive direction. It's what we choose to do with our anger that will determine the impact of it in our lives and in the lives of those around us.

Early in his reign, King Saul channeled his anger into a powerful force for good. The justice and provision of

God roared down the river of Saul's righteous anger to inflict defeat upon the enemy and bring victory for God's people.

The barbaric Ammonite tribe had laid siege to the Israelite town of Jabesh-Gilead. God's people were surrounded and afraid. Adding to the terror was the demand of the Ammonite leader Nahash to gouge out every right eye of the Israelites in exchange for mercy. Nahash had no idea that this heinous offer of a peace treaty had lit a fuse of righteous anger in Saul to defend his kingdom.

When Saul heard their words, the Spirit of God came powerfully upon him, and he burned with anger. (1 Samuel 11:6 NIV)

There it is. The water is starting to boil. And the fire beneath the pot is being stoked by God Himself. You see, some of us have mistakenly believed that anger in any form is evil. But when anger is harnessed and given direction, it can be the motivation and passion needed to accomplish great things.

Again, it's a lot like water. Rivers have been used to transport people and cargo throughout history. Modern technology has enabled us to utilize the power of water to produce electricity. When water is heated to the point of steam, it can be used to propel ships. In the same way, when our anger is controlled and aligned with God, it becomes a powerfully productive force to accomplish His purposes.

[CONTROL AND ALIGNMENT]

⁵but for Cain and his offering he had no regard. So Cain was very angry, and his face fell. ⁶The Lord said to Cain, "Why are you angry, and why has your face fallen? ⁷If you do well, will you not be accepted? And if you do not do well, sin is crouching at the door. Its desire is contrary to you, but you must rule over it." (Genesis 4:5-7 ESV)

The first time Scripture references anger in humanity is in the story of Cain and Abel. Both Cain and Abel offered sacrifices to God. Abel's sacrifice pleased God, but Cain's offering was rejected. While the specifics of why God didn't accept Cain's offering are not given, it's clear there was some kind of disobedience—either in the nature of Cain's offering or in the condition of his heart.

Cain becomes angry over the rejection of his offering, and God lovingly warns him, and all of us, that sin is like a predator waiting to pounce and overtake us. We will either rule over our sin, or it will rule over us and wreak havoc in our lives. Cain's unrepentant heart and uncontrolled anger will eventually lead him to murder his brother. When we don't deal with our anger, it allows the enemy to gain ground in our lives.

Like water that's gone rogue, out of control anger is a dangerous thing. Just ask the residents along the Mississippi River who've experienced its destructive flood waters. From tsunamis to monsoons, water without direction is deadly. Uncontrolled anger works the same way. It destroys marriages and families. It splits churches and ends ministries. It leads to regrettable decisions and downfalls.

On the other hand, when our anger is surrendered to God, it becomes a strength rather than a weakness. It can move us from the spectator stands into the arena to fight the battles we're meant to fight. It becomes a passion that can motivate us to action on issues near and dear to the heart of God.

> *9And they said to the messengers who had come, "Thus shall you say to the men of Jabesh-Gilead: 'Tomorrow, by the time the sun is hot, you shall have salvation.'" When the messengers came and told the men of Jabesh, they were glad. (1 Samuel 11:9 ESV)*

> *11And the next day Saul put the people in three companies. And they came into the midst of the camp in the morning watch and struck down the Ammonites until the heat of the day. And those who survived were scattered, so that no two of them were left together." (1 Samuel 11:11 ESV)*

Saul's righteous anger to defend God's people fueled his victory over the enemy and his obedience to God. As he brought his anger under God's control and in alignment with God's purpose, he was in a position to be used greatly. Saul was moved to anger over the right things, and it led him to fight the right battles.

> *And Saul was very angry, and this saying displeased him. He said, "They have ascribed to David ten thousands, and to me they have ascribed thousands, and what more can he have but the kingdom?" (1 Samuel 18:8 ESV)*

Unfortunately, Saul would allow his righteous river of anger to dam up, creating a barrier between his heart and God.

The victory over the Ammonites would dissipate into the fog of history as the sun rose on a different day and a different Saul. As Saul fearfully forfeited his duty to defend Israel against the Philistine giant to a shepherd boy, the dark battle brewing in Saul's soul intensified. Now, in a state of sin and compromise, Saul will allow his anger over David's fame to stew until it morphs into a bitterness that will eventually consume his life.

Much like the stagnant pond water I swallowed as a kid, when we drink the poison of bitterness it becomes septic to our souls and harmful to those around us.

Saul will allow his bitterness to destroy his life. While David was completely devoted to Saul, he will spend years on the run to save his life from the angry and bitter king. The righteous anger that led Saul to wield the sword against Israel's enemies was now the rage that would cause him to hurl his spear at an innocent young man.

Saul's anger drove away his family and nearly killed his son, Jonathan. When anger is out of control, everyone is affected.

> *But now you must put them all away: anger, wrath, malice, slander, and obscene talk from your mouth. (Colossians 3:8 ESV)*

The anger we're commanded to put away in Colossians isn't righteous anger. The anger referred to in this verse is characteristic of a disobedient heart. It's the anger that we leave unchecked and allow to turn into toxic bitterness or explosive rage.

Just like with every struggle in our lives, the antidote to our anger problem is to place it under the authority of God. We must confront it rather than ignore it. We must confess it rather than justify it. We must allow God to illuminate the source of our anger so that we don't remain in this destructive cycle and end up like Saul—diminished, defeated, and ultimately denied the plan that God had for us.

Chapter Eight
The Deception of Jealousy

[7]And the women sang to one another as they celebrated, "Saul has struck down his thousands, and David his ten thousands. [8]And Saul was very angry, and this saying displeased him. He said, "They have ascribed to David ten thousands, and to me they have ascribed thousands, and what more can he have but the kingdom?" [9]And Saul eyed David from that day on. (1 Samuel 18:7-9 ESV)

The presidential election of 1912 was one of the most fascinating in American history. While most elections for America's top political office involve a campaign between two major-party candidates, this election turned the political norm upside down.

Former President Theodore Roosevelt, endearingly nicknamed Teddy, was already the most famous man in the world when he decided to "throw his hat in the ring" for this 3-way race for the White House.

Roosevelt's life and career are among some of the

most interesting of anyone in U.S. history. He was a Harvard graduate, prolific writer, successful statesman, and decorated war hero. He served as Governor of New York and Vice President of the United States before becoming the youngest person to assume the presidency at only 42 years of age. With the assassination of President William McKinley, Roosevelt was thrust from what he felt was the most boring job on earth to the most powerful position in the world. He would serve two terms as one of the most beloved and successful chief executives in history and would eventually be memorialized on Mount Rushmore as one of our country's most influential leaders.[1]

Always the rugged outdoorsman and adventurer, when Roosevelt left the White House in 1908, he embarked on a 10-month African hunting safari and European tour that captivated the American public. When he arrived in New York Harbor almost two years later, one of the largest parades in the city's history awaited him. The hero was home. What no one realized at the time was, the hero wasn't finished.

Never one to be easily satisfied and quite young in only his mid-50s, Roosevelt's restless mind and endless energy thrust him back onto the political stage almost immediately. Roosevelt felt that his hand-picked replacement, William Howard Taft, had done a disappointing job as president. Many of the achievements of the Roosevelt administration were losing ground, and Roosevelt felt his legacy was on the line.

With the 1912 election looming and the brilliant college president and Democrat nominee Woodrow Wilson threatening to take the White House from Republicans, Roosevelt decided to enter the race. When his own Republican party used back door logistics to keep the nomination from falling to him, Roosevelt started an independent political party—the Progressive Party. Adding to the irresistible narrative of this election, the party was nicknamed the "Bull Moose Party," based on the claim the former president often made that he was "strong as a bull moose."

While the campaign itself was a huge success for Roosevelt, he ultimately lost the election to Wilson, but still holds the record for the highest number of votes received by any third-party candidate in a presidential race.

But a few years after the election, those closest to the dynamic leader watched as he grew increasingly bitter over the loss.[2] When the first World War broke out on President Wilson's watch, Roosevelt's discontentment and resentment over the office he no longer held began to intensify. He believed, and most experts agreed, that he was far more qualified to lead the country during wartime.

Over the course of the next few years, Roosevelt found every way conceivable to take pot shots at President Wilson. As the more beloved of the two, he used his connection with the populace to criticize the sitting president. As the more experienced, he used his knowledge to shame his former opponent. As the more masterful communicator, he verbally bullied Wilson in speeches and in editorials.

In an illustrious career that is still esteemed to this day, this was not Roosevelt's finest moment. But, as one of my personal leadership heroes, he may have taught me one of his strongest lessons through it. Watch out for jealousy—it can get the best and brightest among us.

> *Wrath is cruel, anger is overwhelming, but who can stand before jealousy? (Proverbs 27:4 ESV)*

The song of the Israelite women made David smile but King Saul seethe with envy. It didn't matter to him that their song of celebration had included the king—jealousy leaves room for no one else.

At this point in the story, King Saul was an established monarch with years under his crown and victories under his belt. Secure leaders are able to encourage and champion younger ones because they understand mentorship is vital to the future of their organization. But Israel's king was not secure.

Saul should have wrapped his muscled arm around David's neck and thanked him for defeating the giant on his behalf. Saul could have looked stronger than ever if he had publicly acknowledged and approved of David, but jealousy blinds us to the blessings in our life. Although he gladly shared the battlefield with David, he was unwilling to share the victory song.

Saul's issues must have been obvious to David early on, but there is no indication in Scripture that David ever attempted to undermine King Saul's authority. In fact, he did just the opposite. David used his talents and abilities to serve his king. After God's rejection of Saul, bitterness began to harden his heart and erode his life. It was in these moments of depression that David, who was also a skilled musician, would play soothing music to calm Saul. When Saul needed a military victory, it was David who picked up the sword and went to battle for him. When Saul called, David answered. But jealousy made it impossible for Saul to appreciate the blessing David was to his life and kingdom.

You see, Saul saw in David a picture of what he himself could have been. David was a constant reminder to Saul of his own failure as king. He knew that God had removed His blessing from his life, and so the favor of God that David experienced caused Saul's resentment to grow.

The tragic thing is, Saul still had the crown. God had spared his life. By grace, Saul was still on the throne, which meant the pen of history was still spilling its ink on the pages of Saul's life story. Saul could have written one of the most poignant and inspiring stories of redemption, restoration, and self-sacrifice recorded in Scripture. Saul had an opportunity to repent, to make a difference, and to leave a legacy. Instead, he chose to allow his failure and the regret of what he'd lost to rob him of the future that was still possible.

Jealousy is an insidious sin that cries out, "I want what you have, and, furthermore, I don't want you to have it." It replaces contentment with resentment and spawns a myriad of other sins. Saul wanted David's talent, confidence, and status. And he certainly didn't want David to have any of it.

What he failed to grasp was that David had paid a price Saul was unwilling to pay. David had been obedient to God even when it was difficult. David had courageously fought the battles that he was meant to fight. David had honored and submitted to the authorities God had placed in his life, including King Saul. He didn't have to kick open doors; he simply walked confidently through the ones God opened for him. David's life exhibited the qualities of a contented heart that we as believers are called to as well.

> *Not that I am speaking of being in need, for I have learned in whatever situation I am to be content. (Philippians 4:11 ESV)*

In our culture today, the term "contentment" can evoke different ideas depending on the context. We use it to refer to peace and happiness, but it can also have a negative connotation in reference to someone who's satisfied to remain in mediocrity or stuck in poor circumstances. And we most often use it when we talk about "stuff."

But in actuality, biblical contentment has little to do with our material possessions or even our place in life. The contentment that the apostle Paul talks about in Philippians is an inner fulfillment found only in Christ.

Paul had been rich, and he had been poor. He had

been both a respected intellectual leader in the community and a despised outsider to the religious norms of his day. He had been free, and he had been in prison. He had been well fed but had also suffered horrific hunger. And with this broad life experience, Paul had learned by the grace of God to be content *in* all things.

Don't miss this. Paul didn't say he was content *with* all things. Biblical contentment is not complacency. Paul obviously wasn't thrilled *with* his circumstances. He didn't *like* the prison he'd been unjustly thrown into. He asked the churches to pray for his release. But Paul trusted Jesus to be his source of contentment *in* the prison.

The person in a struggling marriage can remain committed and content *in* the marriage while still working to address the problems *with* the marriage. We can be faithful *in* our current job while doing the hard work required for a new career. We can find peace in the middle of a crisis while trusting in God's promises and provision. Biblical contentment enables us to stand strong in any situation, while also giving us the strength to better our lives.

See, contentment doesn't mean we don't work to improve our lives—it means we can have peace and fulfillment no matter where we are in the process. It enables us to live in gratitude and steward our current season of life well. It frees us from the frustration of constantly trying to gauge how we measure up compared to those around us. Contentment allows us to live securely because it trusts in God's plan for *our* life.

Instead of being content and secure in God, Saul actively tried to destroy the person who embodied the life he believed belonged to him. Rather than working to tell a great story with the life God had given him, he decided to seek to sabotage the one God had given David. Being jealous of someone else's life is never going to improve our own.

No one wants to admit jealousy can be an issue, but it's something we have to guard against most every day, especially in a culture driven by social media.

If you are wondering how to identify jealousy in your own life, just examine the way you speak about other people. When you hear of someone else's success, do you attempt to explain it away? Does it make you feel dissatisfied in your own life or somehow slighted by God?

The writer of Hebrews admonishes us as believers to run the race God has set before us.[3] One of the surest ways to fall during a race is to set our eyes on those around us instead of on the finish line. We each have a race to run. God has designed a unique plan for each of our lives. Let's not allow ourselves to be tripped up by jealousy. Let's celebrate the lives of others and be grateful for the blessings in our own, all the while remaining deeply committed to making the changes needed to live a life worthy of our calling in Christ.

Chapter Nine
The Ripple Effect

I was blessed to have had an amazing grandfather. I've often thought that if every boy could've had a grandfather like I had—a "Pop"—the world would be a very different place. Pop had a big personality that was magnetic to a boy like me. As he was never one to sit around, my time with him always included some sort of outdoor adventure often involving tractors, four-wheelers, guns for either hunting or shooting sporting clays, or a fishing rod. Yep, I had a cowboy for a Pop.

Pop and I spent a great deal of time fishing. He taught me many things, but one beautiful morning at one of the ponds on his property, he taught me one I'd never forget—ripple effect.

Pop loved all kinds of fishing, but nothing brought him more enjoyment than top-water baits. Top-water fishing involves the use of a bait that floats rather than one that sinks below the water's surface. What makes top-water fishing so fun is the moment the fish strikes; it becomes an exciting explosion rather than just a sinking cork or tug on your line. It's awesome! The go-to lure for my Pop was an interesting contraption he called the "ole devil horse." Now, being a strong Christian, this name had nothing to do with the enemy of our souls but everything to do with the ability of this artificial bait to look so tempting to a largemouth bass that the creature just couldn't resist. The devil's horse lure was basically a long and slender minnow painted black on top and white on the bottom with yellow eyes and four hooks that hung below its belly from nose to tail. Now, the look of the bait was certainly important, but as I learned that day at the pond, the real magic was in how you used the devil's horse on the top of the water.

Standing on the muddy bank with a light breeze dancing through the pines that stood proud behind us, Pop taught me how to properly use his choice lure. First, he let out a little line from the tip of the rod allowing the bait to hang and move freely—but not too much. Then, with a long sweeping motion he brought the rod back behind his shoulders and whipped it forward while simultaneously pointing the rod in the desired direction and releasing the button on the reel that lets out the line. I can still hear his deep Mississippi drawl as the words came out just a bit above a whisper so the fish wouldn't be spooked. I eagerly watched as the "ole devil horse" flew through the humid air and hit the glassy surface with a splash. Then, according to Pop, came the crucial part.

"Ok, son, when the bait hits the water, don't move it

at all. See all the ripples it just made? Just sit back and wait until they are all gone. When the water is smooth again, start moving the bait. Give it a little jerk, then reel it three or four times. Another quick jerk, then another few reels. And, bud, get ready, cause he's coming to get it!"

He went on to explain that this approach made the artificial minnow appear to be injured and easy pickings for the bass. The secret was in having the patience to let those ripples smooth out. When the bait hits the water with that splash, it initially scares the fish, causing them to quickly back down in the water in order to investigate. Moving the lure too soon causes the fish to move on rather than take the bite. But if you wait for the ripple effect to play out, the fish settle down and go from fearful to curious. When the devil's horse finally moves, it's game time because that bass is coming for dinner.

This fishing instruction had a built-in physics lesson. When an object is thrown into a body of water, no matter the size of the object, it causes a ripple effect. Water is suddenly displaced, and energy is produced that often manifests as small ripples moving across the water in all directions away from the point of impact. Everything around the impact zone is affected in some way.

The ripple effect is a very real thing in water, and I've found that it's a very real thing in life. Observing the life of King Saul from the shores of history, we can clearly see the ripple effect in action as his family, friends, and coun-trymen feel the impact of his decisions. Saul seemed to see life through the myopic lens of how things would go for himself, never others. But, the ripple effect leaves no one untouched.

[THE ARMY]

> The battle extended beyond Beth-aven, [24]and the men of Israel were worn out that day, for Saul had placed the troops under an oath: "the man who eats food before evening, before I have taken vengeance on my enemies is cursed." So none of the troops tasted any food. (1 Samuel 14:24 CSB)

In the middle of another heated battle with the Philistine army, Saul sets the ripple effect in motion with an impulsive and devastating military decision. In a sheer moment of bravado, Saul ordered that his men not be allowed to eat until the battle was won. Don't miss his motivation here, which is revealed to us by the spotlight of Scripture—self-exaltation. He wants *his* vengeance. It's all about *Saul*.

This decision was not only selfish but foolish. An army caught in a fierce battle desperately needs *energy*. One can imagine the nutritional depletion that takes place inside the body of a warrior during a deadly and prolonged battle. This self-centered king was starving his men to death when they needed sustenance the most. In his desire to look strong and victorious, Saul did not fully consider how this decision would impact his army.

You see, the ripples caused by our decisions never

impact us alone. Sometimes, the ripples are positive. Unfortunately, for those closest to Saul, the ripples left behind from this decision—and many others—would harm more than help. And in this case, it almost cost Saul's son his life.

[THE SON]

> ²⁵Now when all the people came to the forest, behold, there was honey on the ground. ²⁶And when the people entered the forest, behold, the honey was dropping, but no one put his hand to his mouth, for the people feared the oath. ²⁷But Jonathan had not heard his father charge the people with the oath, so he put out the tip of the staff that was in his hand and dipped it in the honeycomb and put his hand to his mouth, and his eyes became bright. ²⁸Then one of the people said, "Your father strictly charged the people with an oath, saying, 'Cursed be the man who eats food this day.'" And the people were faint. (1 Samuel 14:25-28 ESV)

Jonathan had not heard his father's ridiculous proclamation, so when he found the honey, he quickly turned his staff into a spoon and partook. This was nature's energy drink, so Jonathan was immediately strengthened. The sugar had barely hit his depleted blood stream when he was informed by a terrified comrade of the potentially fatal mistake he'd just unknowingly made.

29 Then Jonathan said, "My father has troubled the land. See how my eyes have become bright because I tasted a little of this honey. 30 How much better if the people had eaten freely today of the spoil of their enemies that they found. For now the defeat among the Philistines has not been great." (1 Samuel 14:29-30 ESV)

It must have been difficult for Jonathan to admit that his father was a questionable leader. I think all children are born with a hard-wiring to admire and imitate their parents. I can remember in kindergarten getting into an argument with a classmate about how tall our dads were. Before it was over, both our fathers had grown to mythic proportions. An inevitable part of life is realizing that your parents are human and will make mistakes, too. Sadly, in Jonathan's case, he doesn't just have an imperfect father—he has a destructive one.

Jonathan, by all biblical accounts, was a man any father would have been proud to call a son. Loyal, capable, and brave, this young man was respected and loved. Saul, on the other hand, was a father who made the fatal mistake of placing his job before his parenting. He made decisions that time and again would cause great hardship for his son. When Saul became a king, he seemed to forget that he was first and foremost a father. He made this royal edict without considering the implications, not only for his exhausted army, but also for his loyal son.

⁴³Then Saul said to Jonathan, "Tell me what you have done." And Jonathan told him, "I tasted a little honey with the tip of the staff that was in my hand. Here I am; I will die." ⁴⁴And Saul said, "God do so to me and more also; you shall surely die, Jonathan." ⁴⁵Then the people said to Saul, "Shall Jonathan die, who has worked this great salvation in Israel? Far from it! As the Lord lives, there shall not one hair of his head fall to the ground, for he has worked with God this day." So the people ransomed Jonathan, so that he did not die. (1 Samuel 14:43-45 ESV)

Amazingly, Saul was so stubborn and committed to his own prestige that he was more than willing to have his son put to death. Reading the story of Saul's life, we see that there were many opportunities for him to change, moments that could have and should have mattered. This is one of them. This should have awakened Saul to the issues that were slowly tearing him and his world apart. This was not a time to dig in his heels; this was a time for repentance. The people, not Saul, rescued Jonathan. It must have stung to the core for this loyal son to realize his father's reputation meant more to him than Jonathan's own life.

Be warned by this story. We often make the same mistake of prioritizing the wrong things in our lives. In a culture where we idolize success and status, our most important relationships often suffer. In our selfish pursuits, we often starve those in our lives who need us the most.

And Saul will continue to make life difficult for his son. When the legendary giant slayer David comes onto the scene, he and Jonathan become best friends. Jonathan loved David so purely that he seemed to have no jealousy whatsoever that David, not him, would eventually become the king. When King Saul goes on a prolonged attack against David, Jonathan will have to continually protect his dear friend from his increasingly unstable father. I can only imagine the pain of a son who must work against his father rather than alongside him.

My grandfather told me a story once that I've always remembered. When he was a teenager, his father became an alcoholic and was separated from his wife and family. One day, he showed up at their home drunk and belligerent and attempted to physically assault his wife—the woman who would one day become my great-grandmother. My Pop, as a young man, ran to her rescue. Standing in between his father and mother, he threatened to strike his father if he continued his assault. His dad angrily backed away and left. At this point in the telling of the story, my Pop gazed off into the distance as he softly said, "If I would have hit my daddy that day, I would have been useless the rest of my life." Thankfully, my great-grandparents eventually reconciled, and the relationship between my great-grandfather and my Pop was restored. But I'll always remember the way my Pop told that story. That moment had a haunting impact on him. No son wants to come against his father. My Pop didn't. Jonathan didn't. But Saul forced him to.

Saul's malice toward David, and the ripples this would create across the surface of his life, would extend beyond Jonathan. Saul's daughter will marry David only to watch her father chase him like a wild animal for years. In his unquenchable anger, Saul will have eighty-five loyal priests executed because he felt they helped David escape. The prophet Samuel will remain in constant frustration and disappointment over Saul's insolence and stubbornness. The Bible tells us that he will end up in a state of mourning over Saul's broken kingdom. Saul allowed his issues to turn him into a hideous monster rather than a regal monarch. The ripples in Saul's life transformed from small disturbances to massive waves of carnage, intensifying as they moved unhindered toward others.

David, the future king, will spend a decade running from a king he loved. He will have numerous opportunities to kill Saul and end the whole debacle, but his integrity won't allow it. David waits patiently for God to give him the throne while avoiding the relentless rage of the king with the broken crown.

[LEGACY]

At a time in his life when Saul should have been enjoying the memories of a glorious reign as king, he instead allowed the ripple effect to push him into an embarrassingly desperate position. Saul should have been enjoying the grandchildren given to him by Jonathan and David.

Can you picture it? The whole family sitting happily around the royal table laughing and reminiscing, with David learning from Saul as he prepares to pass the torch of leadership to the young man who he has personally mentored. This is how the story could have ended, but Saul just couldn't let go of his resentment. Running out of ways to vent his anger and becoming increasingly vulnerable to his enemies, we find King Saul across the table from a delusional witch instead.

> *5When Saul saw the army of the Philistines, he was afraid, and his heart trembled greatly. 6And when Saul inquired of the Lord, the Lord did not answer him, either by dreams, or by Urim, or by prophets. 7Then Saul said to his servants, "Seek out for me a woman who is a medium, that I may go to her and inquire of her." And his servants said to him, "Behold, there is a medium at En-dor." 8So Saul disguised himself and put on other garments and went, he and two men with him. And they came to the woman by night. And he said, "Divine for me by a spirit and bring up for me whomever I shall name to you." (1 Samuel 28:5-8 ESV)*

Hiding out in a dusty tent, Saul disobeys God again as he seeks to find answers to what has become his mess of a life. There's great debate as to who exactly the witch of Endor called up to speak to Saul, but she's as surprised and terrified as he is. Some theologians believe God supernaturally allowed Samuel the prophet to speak to

Saul from the grave. Whatever or whomever it was, the message was a true one, and it was a message Saul didn't want to hear. The ripples were now a tsunami, and it was too late to avoid the coming disaster. Saul, his family, and his kingdom were about to be swept away by the waves that began long before.

When we run from God, we always regret it. Allowing our ripples to go unnoticed and unchanged will place us in a state of desperation, leading us to think and do things unimaginable. That's where Saul finds himself as he cries out to God for answers instead of forgiveness. Saul wants God to rescue his reputation instead of his heart. He's looking for an external victory instead of an internal rescue. God was willing and ready to change Saul's heart. He is for us as well. But, praying the wrong prayer can be devastating. God did not answer Saul. You can feel the cold silence through the ancient pages. Nothing. I've felt that, too. I prayed for God to grow my ministry when I should have asked Him to grow my character. I've prayed for Him to change the hearts of others when I should have asked Him to change mine.

Saul was asking for victory over the wrong enemy. It wasn't the dangerous Philistine army Saul should have feared the most. It was the enemy he'd refused to face for decades. It was the one wearing the increasingly tainted crown. Saul's real enemy was himself.

What about me and you? I bet you can see ripples in your life that need to be stopped now. Unlike Saul, we still have time to change our stories. More importantly,

God can change our stories. Many of us are creating our own ripples with our current habits, attitudes, and decisions, and these ripples often affect our loved ones. Jonathan and his brother will die with their father. His servant will come to a violent end. Untold numbers of Israelites will suffer under the hand of the Philistines. All a result of Saul's ripple effect. Let's use Saul's example and change the story while we still can.

Chapter Ten
A Regrettable Ending

Most people have a deep fear of death. Even for many of us who have faith in God, there is still a touch of dread when it comes to our last breath. This is probably because, as creatures made in the image of the Living God, we intrinsically know death wasn't meant for us. We realize it wasn't supposed to be this way. Human rebellion led us to the inevitable reality of death. Scripture tells us that we have all sinned and fallen short of the perfect standards of God. Like Adam and Eve before us, we have all bitten of the forbidden fruit, rebelling against our Creator.

I think the thing that scares us the most is not so much death itself, but how exactly we will die. It is quite an interesting thing to listen to a person describe the way they hope to go in the end, isn't it? My grandfather didn't want anyone to see him die, and we didn't. He took his last breath while no one was in the room with him after a long battle with heart disease. My aunt beautifully said, "Pop snuck off to heaven when we weren't looking just like he hoped."

Now, my grandmother, who we affectionately called "Nanny," was a different story.

When it came to death, she did not want to be alone. By God's grace, just a few years after the love of her life went to be with Jesus, Nanny peacefully stepped into eternity with me and my dad holding one hand and her daughter, son-in-law, and granddaughter holding the other. It was a beautiful exit for a beautiful lady.

Like my grandparents, if we are Christians, where we go after our deaths has been completely settled in Christ. Therefore, the most important question about our ending becomes not how we will go, but this—what have we left behind? Can those behind us follow the trail we blazed forward? Thankfully, while not perfect, my grandparents left a legacy of a family who loves God and each other. We have more good memories than we can count. While the world will never know them, our family will never forget them. They left a good legacy. And that's the choice we have, too. What kind of legacy are we leaving behind with our decisions?

The mighty Philistines never stopped in their quest to destroy Israel and make an example of their arrogant king. Saul's relentless pursuit of David had taken his focus away from Israel's true enemy, and while Israel depleted their resources to appease the vengeful ego of their king, the Philistines were preparing to take full advantage of this self-inflicted vulnerability. The epic battle that closes the book of 1 Samuel is the one that will end Saul's life.

The only thing worse than how Saul dies is the legacy he leaves behind.

> ³*The battle pressed hard against Saul, and the archers found him, and he was badly wounded by the archers. ⁴Then Saul said to his armor-bearer, "Draw your sword, and thrust me through with it, lest these uncircumcised come and thrust me through, and mistreat me." But his armor-bearer would not, for he feared greatly. Therefore Saul took his own sword and fell upon it. ⁵And when his armor-bearer saw that Saul was dead, he also fell upon his sword and died with him.*
> (1 Samuel 31:3-5 ESV)

Decades before at his coronation, Saul stood in a pool of his own sweat produced by the fear and insecurity that paralyzed him initially but would come to perpetually drive him later in his life. On his last day, Saul stood paralyzed again—only this time, in a pool of his own blood. Nowhere to run, no army to help, and no slingshot wielding country boy to save the day—no, Saul had made sure of that. This was a situation he was forced to own. Sure, the Philistines shot the arrows, but Saul gave them the target, and they struck the king with deadly accuracy. I can imagine that, as he stood in that moment of defeat, the agonizing pain of the arrows piercing his body couldn't compare to the pain of a lifetime of regret suddenly rushing in around him like a flood.

King Saul never willingly chose the shameful way

his life ended, but he had been choosing his legacy for decades with his actions. For forty years, he'd worn a crown that he slowly broke. For forty years, he ruled over a kingdom he gradually weakened. Forty years is a long time. There were many times that Saul could have changed for the good of those who loved and followed him. A life that should have ended in a triumphant celebration of a forty-year reign became one of the most painful memories in the history of Israel. Their first king—regal, handsome, and strong—dies by falling on his own sword.

Saul's final command as a king was rejected, which must have been a reminder to him of how far he'd fallen. So, with a vile enemy coming in and a terrified servant watching, the first king of Israel took his own life. Sadly, but fittingly, Saul's last living act was lethal, and the initial impact of his legacy was as well.

Thus Saul died, and his three sons, and his armor-bearer, and all his men, on the same day together. (1 Samuel 31:6 ESV)

In one poignant sentence, 1 Samuel 31:6 somberly summarizes the day Saul died. With three dead sons and an army closing in on him, Saul's life was coming to the end. With the ripple effect in full motion, Saul's tragic ending engulfs those around him as well. Before the archers of the enemy set their mark on Israel's king, they get his boys. Jonathan. Abinadab. Malchishua. The royal trio. Men with families and stories of their own, with wives and children they loved, and with communities of friends they enjoyed. Their father never earned their loyalty, but he would have it to the end. The sons of Saul fought for him and their country to the death. The enemy that Saul should have prepared for was the one who would defeat him and his loved ones.

> *For we do not wrestle against flesh and blood, but against the rulers, against the authorities, against the cosmic powers over this present darkness, against the spiritual forces of evil in the heavenly places.*
> *(Ephesians 6:12 ESV)*

One thing I'm convinced of is that you and I have a real enemy and we are in a battle. To neglect to prepare for this battle will have deadly consequences in our lives, too.

Like Goliath in the valley before the Israelites, your enemy will meet you every day. So, what are the giants in your life? What or who is the real threat that you need to zero in on? As a husband, I know the enemy is taking aim at my marriage. As a father, I can see the evil army in battle formation against my children. As a pastor, I can hear the battle drums beating every day as the forces of evil seek to hinder the forward march of God's Church. If you're like me, you know where the real battle is, but you find yourself fighting the wrong one sometimes. We fight against our spouses when we should be building them up. We fight against our kids when we should be lovingly guiding them. We go to battle with those in our churches rather than joining with them in battle against the true enemy. Choosing to fight the wrong battle for too long left Saul and Israel susceptible to a deadly attack, and it will do the same for us.

Like Saul, the biggest enemy some of us are facing right now is the one staring back at us in the mirror. Rather than boldly confronting the enemy within, Saul continued to make choices that would cause destruction for those around him. He refused to allow God to excavate his heart, and instead continued to dig pits that those closest to him would fall into.

One of the most selfish things we can do is to deceive ourselves into believing that our decisions today aren't going to affect our loved ones tomorrow. If you're a parent, your children are following your lead, for better or worse. If you're a teacher, you have unbelievable influence on your students that can be positive or negative. If you're a pastor, understand that your character will have a greater impact on those around you than the eloquence of your words.

Although Saul avoided giving the Philistines the satisfaction of taking his life, his sons would end up dying in the trenches their father had been digging for decades with his decisions. King Saul teaches us in defeat a lesson that could bring us victory if we heed its warning. It's time to put down the shovel and stop digging. It's time to pick up the sword and start fighting the right battles. Confront the things in your life that are causing setbacks rather than advancements. Your life is depending on it. The lives of your loved ones are, too.

Behold, I have acted foolishly, and have made a great mistake. (1 Samuel 26:21 ESV)

King Saul made this statement in a sobering moment of clarity before taking his final sinful plunge toward the end of his story. It may have been the most authentic moment of his life. Make no mistake, we are choosing today the legacy we will leave tomorrow. Reading Saul's story must do more for us than simply give us a sad history lesson of Israel's foray into a monarchy. God had this story recorded in the holy pages of Scripture to help us, warn us, and guide us. This story was meant to help change our stories. We have so much in common with King Saul. We have the same sin disease infecting us that brought him to his fateful end.

I agree with the majority of theologians who believe that, while Saul's story is tragic, his soul was secure. So, if you are a believer in Christ, you will get to meet Israel's first king one day. Oh, the stories I bet he'll tell of God's grace in his life and how he received, in Eternity, what he never earned or deserved. This, my friends, will be our story as well.

But, the point of this book is to make sure that's the only part of King Saul's story we share. Because God lovingly recorded in painful but helpful detail this epic tale for us, we can change our stories on this side of the grave. With Saul as a guide, it's time to pick up our pens and start writing better stories. Gospel stories. God's story.

Chapter Eleven
The One True King

For a child will be born to us, a son will be given to us; and the government will rest on His shoulders; and His name will be called Wonderful Counselor, Mighty God, Eternal Father, Prince of Peace. (Isaiah 9:6 CSB)

Fear not, daughter of Zion; behold, your king is coming, sitting on a donkey's colt! (John 12:15 ESV)

It was much too early on a Friday morning for the highest-ranking official in Judea. Pilate was a man known for his quick temper and brutality. The Jewish people had been nothing but a problem for him from the moment the power hub of Rome decided to place him in charge of their geographical area. As the Roman Empire expanded its borders, leaders like Pilate were called up to keep the peace in the occupied territory while keeping the money flowing to Rome. Pilate, like most Romans, was a superstitious man with pagan tendencies. He knew there was something or someone in control—a higher power of some sort—but a gnawing curiosity and uncertainty pervaded his mind. He's about to meet a man that he'll never forget.

Jesus of Nazareth had been causing a stir in Jerusalem for a week. Pilate had been informed of the massive crowds and extraordinary miracles that allegedly followed Jesus wherever He went. And this was making him nervous. He didn't need another uprising to force his hand. He didn't need more crucifixions under his command to incite the already fierce ire of this uber-religious group of people. His authorities had already put him on notice that if he couldn't keep the Jews under control, they would find someone who could. His handling of what he faced this Friday morning could have huge consequences for his future.

Jesus looked like an ordinary young Jewish man as he was violently dragged before Pilate. His face was badly bruised, and chunks of his beard had clearly been torn away and left bleeding. Pilate was now sitting in what they called the "seat of judgment," so his mind was already spinning. *Who was this man? Why were the Jews so angry?* The context of the moment only increased his desire to get this right.

Because torture and crucifixion were more often than not the fate of those who stood before Pilate, it created an environment of terror. The Jews also saw Pilate as the face of their occupation from Rome, so he disgusted them. Those subject to Pilate's judgment seat simultaneously displayed fear and anger. Interestingly, when his eyes met those of Jesus for the first time, neither anger nor disgust were present. He wasn't sure anyone had ever looked at him like Jesus did. This was no normal prisoner, and this would not be a normal Friday.

Complicating matters, Pilate is interrupted by an urgent message from his wife. *Why is she up this early? What could be so important that she'd send the message now?* Bad timing for sure. As he listens to the servant whisper the message in his ear, his heart begins to flutter and beads of sweat form on his forehead as anxiety overtakes him. She says she's had a dream about the Jewish man standing in front of him and warns Pilate to leave Jesus alone. For a man like Pilate, this was extremely disconcerting. Initially, Jesus piqued Pilate's interest. Now, He is making Pilate uncomfortable.

One of the most fascinating conversations in all of the Bible takes place between this Roman governor and the Jewish Messiah. Jesus is firm but kind. He is not condescending to Pilate but allows the full weight of simple truth to rest on Pilate's intellect and heart. Pilate finds himself talking to a prisoner about the deepest questions of his life. *What is truth? Does it even exist? Why is a powerful Roman official having a philosophical dialogue with a battered criminal?* Pilate finds himself wanting to ask Jesus more questions. *There's something about this man.* Pilate pulls himself together. He doesn't have time for this. The angry Jewish leaders before him are demanding answers. He has to do something. So, he asks Jesus a question.

> *Then Pilate said to Him, "So you are a king?"* (*John 18:37 ESV*)

The most important question a human can ask is "Who is Jesus?" The answer to this question is the hinge upon which the door of all history—past, present, and future—swings. It is the key that unlocks the door of eternity. Who is Jesus? Pilate got to ask Him this crucial question face-to-face.

"Who are you? Are you a king? That's what these people say about you. So, Jesus, are you a king? Please tell me your identity."

On this fateful Friday, a pagan Roman official asked the most important person in history the most important question of all time. Pilate got this part right. God alone can reveal Himself to us. We could never find Him on our own. It was God who came for us.

Pilate represents each one of us as he stumbles verbally over the great ponderings of his heart. He's not sure what to make of it all. *Is there anything to truly believe in? What is life all about?* The answer to all of his questions is standing right in front of him, living and breathing. All power encapsulated in a human body, all knowledge held in His holy mind, and all authority at His fingertips. Pilate doesn't know it, but his lungs are breathing the same air as God Himself. And God is about to give him, and all of us, an answer.

Jesus answered, "You say correctly that I am a king, for this I have been born, and for this I have come into the world, to testify to the truth. Everyone who is of the truth hears my voice." (John 18:37 NASB)

King Saul was the first king of Israel, but Jesus is the *true* King of Israel. He's the King of heaven and of earth. And He's the only king worthy to wear the crown.

My mother's side of the family is very creative, and my grandmother was an artist. I loved to sit on her porch and watch her paint the most beautiful landscapes and pictures of nature. She had an amazing ability to bring a blank canvas to life with her oil paints. I picked up the brush as a kid, and as I learned to paint, she taught me the importance of creating contrast. Putting two colors, two shades, or two objects next to each other in contrast, can bring greater clarity and even greater beauty.

In reading about the life of King Saul, you may have wondered why God ever allowed Israel to have an earthly king if it was going to be such a disaster. But that was actually the point. Saul's disappointing reign—and the reigns of all the kings that followed—would provide the needed contrast to reveal the greatness of King Jesus.

[IDENTITY CRISIS VS. SECURE IDENTITY]

We know that King Saul, although privately

confirmed and publicly coronated as king, would never be secure in his God-given identity. Jesus' identity was also both privately and publicly confirmed by God, but unlike Saul, Jesus found His security in who God said He was. Jesus had a private connection with His Father that gave Him public confidence to complete His mission.

It was clear to those closest to Jesus that His power source was His private prayer life. His prayer life was so consistent that Judas knew exactly where to take the mob to arrest Him on the night of His betrayal. God also confirmed Jesus publicly at His baptism. A voice thundered through the Judean skies as the Holy Father spoke of His love for His Son. While the prophet Samuel placed a crown on Saul, the Holy Spirit Himself descended upon Jesus like a dove.

This intimate connection between the Father, Son, and Spirit and public confirmation at His baptism would lay the firm foundation of confidence that would lead Jesus all the way to the cross.

[SELFISHNESS VS. SELFLESSNESS]

True to earthly king form, Saul forced the people of Israel to fight for him. He raised up armies to fight endless battles with the enemies of Israel and, at times, his own perceived enemies. Countless men, young and old, would come to bloody deaths due to the forward march of King Saul. Saul demanded loyalty that would cost people their lives if betrayed.

Jesus would be a different kind of king—a servant king. While most kings demand that people give their lives for the king's honor, Jesus would give his own life to save His people.

[FAILED LEADERSHIP VS. PERFECT LEADERSHIP]

God warned Israel that earthly kings would fail them. Even the good kings of Israel like David and Asa would have moments of failure during their respective reigns.

The leadership of Jesus is perfect. To place our lives under the Crown of Christ is to live the best life possible. Everything Jesus commands is for our good and for His glory. And when He forbids something, it's always for our protection.

> *Come to me, all who labor and are heavy laden, and I will give you rest. 29 Take my yoke upon you, and learn from me, for I am gentle and lowly in heart, and you will find rest for your souls. (Matthew 11:28-29 ESV)*

King Saul's leadership became a heavy weight upon the people of Israel. They suffered under his reign, and in the end, it became clear the choice of an earthly king was regrettable. Jesus' kingship in our lives lifts the burden off of us and gives us rest in return.

[THE BULLY KING VS. THE MEEK KING]

King Saul was a picture of a problem that men have grappled with from the beginning of time. He was an exterior picture of strength and masculinity, but he was a shattered mess inside. The reality did not match the projection. Saul abused his power because his power was out of control.

The Bible describes Jesus as meek. Don't let this word fool you. Meekness is not weakness. Meekness is actually the greatest show of strength. Meekness is *strength under control.* Jesus was the most powerful King, but He harnessed His power for the glory of God and the good of His people.

When Pilate finally threatened Jesus with crucifixion during His trial, Jesus answered him in a way that I'm convinced left Pilate shaking in his boots.

Jesus answered, "You would have no power over me if it were not given to you from above." (John 19:11 NIV)

No one had ever spoken to Pilate like this. With calmness, security, and unmistakable authority, Jesus looks at the Roman governor and tells him that He, not Pilate, is actually the one in charge. After this pivotal moment, Pilate tries to pull off a disappearing act by symbolically washing his hands of Jesus and handing Him over to the Jewish leadership. Like Saul, Pilate wanted power but no responsibility. It would be this brush with ultimate authority that would cause Pilate to momentarily relinquish the power he craved.

Regardless of this feeble move to recuse himself, Jesus' sentencing still fell under the jurisdiction of Pilate—this Roman governor who would never forget the day a Jewish carpenter who claimed to be a king, looked him in the eyes and did not blink.

[A BROKEN KINGDOM VS. THE KINGDOM OF GOD]

Jesus said, "My kingdom is not of this world. If it were, my servants would fight to prevent my arrest by the Jewish leaders. But now my kingdom is from another place." (John 18:36 NIV)

King Saul presided over a broken kingdom, but Jesus' Kingdom will stand strong throughout eternity. While Jesus will one day return to establish His Kingdom on the earth, for now, the Kingdom of God advances in the hearts and lives of His people.

This Kingdom is marked by grace and love. In this Kingdom, we reach and rescue people instead of conquering lands, and we win hearts instead of battles. It's a Kingdom where citizenship was bought by the blood of the King instead of the blood of an army. It's a Kingdom where no one earned their way in, but all gladly serve the King because He graciously welcomed them in.

No, there's never been a kingdom like this Kingdom.

And it's the royal message of this Kingdom—written in the King's own blood—that has changed countless lives.

God made him who had no sin to be sin for us, so that in him we might become the righteousness of God. (2 Corinthians 5:21 NIV)

This King took the place of His people on a cross. This King took the punishment you and I deserved so that we could live forever as royal sons and daughters. This King was broken so that we could be made whole. No, there's never been a king like this King.

The only thing the Romans got right that Friday was the sign that hung above the head of Jesus on the cross. In multiple languages, it read "King of the Jews." Indeed. Jesus was the one true King of Israel, the only King who could restore a broken kingdom and rescue a broken world.

Acknowledgments

I want to thank the staff of 3Circle Church who encouraged me years ago to take a sermon series on King Saul and write a book. You pushed me and helped me turn this idea into a reality.

Thank you to my friend and mentor Larry Osborne for contributing the foreword to *Broken Crown*. Your wisdom is astounding.

Thank you, Keith Glines, for masterminding this project. Your friendship and guidance have been crucial to the production of *Broken Crown*. Stephanie Glines, thank you for polishing my words and being an editor that helped me to find my voice.

To 3Circle Church—leading our dynamic local church is one of the great honors of my life. Local, regional, global is our mission, the gospel is our message, and Jesus is our true King!

Thank you to all the pastors, teachers, coaches, instructors, and professors who have invested in me over the years. I'm forever grateful for your mentorship.

Thank you to my friends—life is rich because of you. The best dirt to grow disciples is biblical community and I'm thankful for the "dirt" God has given me.

Thank you, Mom and Dad, for making sure our little family got to church, youth group, camp, and so much more. Thank you for fanning the flames of my calling as a young man. You led me to the water—I just had to drink!

Thank you, Mike and Darlene, for being like an older brother and sister to me. You've fought your battles well and inspired me along the way.

Thank you, Wendell and Charlotte Barnhill, for the incredible blessing you've been to us. Thank you for loving our family and encouraging our ministry.

Thank you to Terry and Sandra Phillips for being amazing in-laws and encouraging both Nan and me as we fulfill our calling in ministry. Thank you for loving Jesus in front of our entire family.

Thank you to Heath, Nick, and Jeremy. A man could not have better brothers than you guys. Thanks for always having my back, gentlemen.

Thank you, Jill, Deanna, and Britteny for being the sisters I never had—you are all amazing women.

Thank you to my nieces and nephews, collectively known as "the cousins." It's an honor to be your uncle and to watch you grow and follow Jesus.

Thank you to my three wonderful children, Gabe, Cooper, and Gracie. Being your dad is one of the best things in my life. You bring me indescribable joy, and I couldn't be prouder of you.

Most of all, to my beautiful bride, Nan—thank you for loving me and believing in me. More than 20 years ago, we began our adventure together and it has been an amazing journey. I love you more every day.

Notes

Chapter 1- An Environment for Disaster

1. Titanic Facts: The Life & Loss of the RMS Titanic in Numbers. "Titanic Passengers," Accessed March 15, 2019. *https://titanicfacts.net/titanic-passengers/*.

2. Titanic Facts: The Life & Loss of the RMS Titanic in Numbers. "Titanic Sinking." Accessed March 15, 2019. *https://titanicfacts.net/titanic-sinking/*.

3. Titanic Facts: The Life & Loss of the RMS Titanic in Numbers. "Titanic Iceberg." Accessed March 15, 2019. *https://titanicfacts.net/titanic-iceberg/*.

4. Titanic Facts: The Life & Loss of the RMS Titanic in Numbers. "Titanic Victims," Accessed March 15, 2019. *https://titanicfacts.net/titanic-victims/*.

5. Genesis 12.

6. Exodus 3.

7. Exodus 16.

8. Joshua 6.

9. Matthew 6:24

10. Matthew 7:13

Chapter 2 – Little Things Become Big Things

1. Cowherd, Colin, "Monday, November, 21st," The Herd Now, November 21, 2016. *https://www.theherdnow.com/radio/the-packers-are-like-an-80s-rock-band-living-off-their-past-hits/*.

2. Cowherd, Colin, "Monday, November, 21st," The Herd Now. November 21, 2016. *https://www.*

theherdnow.com/radio/the-packers-are-like-an-80s-rock-band-living-off-their-past-hits/
3. Romans 3:23.
4. Matthew 5.

Chapter 3 – The Wrong Fear Choice
1. Proverbs 9:10
2. Proverbs 22:4

Chapter 4 – Impaired Condition
1. History.com Editors, "Tacoma Narrows Bridge collapses," HISTORY, Last updated January 24, 2019, *https://www.history.com/this-day-in-history/tacoma-narrows-bridge-collapses.*
2. Clifford, Howard, "Black and blue and lucky to be alive, the last person to escape Galloping Gertie tells his story," The News Tribune, October 31, 2015, *https://www.thenewstribune.com/news/local/article41608875.html.*
3. John 15:14-15

Chapter 5 – The Pride of Partial Obedience
1. King, Hobart, Ph.D.,RPG. "Tsunami Geology - What Causes a Tsunami?" Geology.com. Accessed March 15, 2019. *https://geology.com/articles/tsunami-geology.shtml.*

Chapter 8 – The Deception of Jealousy
1. Morris, Edmund, Theodore Roosevelt Trilogy Bundle: The Rise of Theodore Roosevelt / Theodore Rex / and Colonel Roosevelt, New York: Random House Publishing Group, 2010.
2. Brands, H.W., T.R.: The Last Romantic, New York: Basic Books, 1997.
3. Hebrews 12:1-2

About the Author

Chris Bell is a dynamic pastor, visionary leader, and passionate teacher, with over 20 years of ministry experience. He is the lead pastor of 3Circle Church, a multisite church along the Gulf Coast of Alabama, named one of the fastest-growing churches in America. Chris loves helping people understand and treasure the Bible, leading them to tangibly impact the world for Christ. He also enjoys speaking at conferences and coaching other pastors and leaders through the Courage to Lead network. Chris studied Theology and Communications at the University of Mobile and Luther Rice Seminary, and is honored to serve as a part of Leadership Alabama, an influential group of community leaders across the state. He and his wife, Nan, have three children: Gabe, Cooper, and Gracie, and love living in beautiful Fairhope, Alabama.